Finding
the
Freedom
of Self-
Control

Finding
the
Freedom
of Self-Control

William Backus

BETHANY HOUSE PUBLISHERS
MINNEAPOLIS, MINNESOTA 55438
A Division of Bethany Fellowship, Inc.

Published by Bethany House Publishers
A Division of Bethany Fellowship, Inc.
6820 Auto Club Road, Minneapolis, Minnesota 55438

Printed in the United States of America

Library of Congress Cataloging-in-Publication Data

Backus, William D.
  Finding the freedom of self-control.

    1. Self-control—Religious aspects—Christianity.
I. Title.
BV4647.S39B33   1987   241'.4   87–1792
ISBN 0–87123–676–1 (pbk.)

To Martin
     Roxanne
        Christa and
          Deborah

Books by Dr. Backus

Finding the Freedom of Self-Control
Finding the Freedom of Self-Control Study Guide (with
      Steven Wiese)
The Paranoid Prophet
Telling Each Other the Truth
Telling the Truth to Troubled People
Telling Yourself the Truth (with Marie Chapian)
Telling Yourself the Truth Study Guide (with Marie Chapian)
Untwisting Twisted Relationships (with Candace Backus)
Why Do I Do What I Don't Want to Do? (with Marie
      Chapian)

Tapes by Dr. Backus

Taking Charge of Your Emotions
Telling Each Other the Truth
Telling Yourself the Truth

WILLIAM BACKUS, Ph.D., is a Christian psychologist and an ordained Lutheran clergyman. He is Founder and Director of the Center for Christian Psychological Services in St. Paul, Minnesota. He and his family make their home in Forest Lake, Minnesota. He is also associate pastor of a large Lutheran church.

The Center for Christian Psychological Services receives numerous requests for referrals to licensed Christian professional counselors who use Christian cognitive therapy as set forth in Dr. Backus' books. The Center would be happy to receive from you a brief summary of your counseling experience with misbelief therapy and your qualifications, license status, and commitment to Christian truth in your practice. On the basis of such information, the Center will refer callers from your area to you. Please include a telephone number with area code, address, and the name of the facility with which you are affiliated.

The Center for Christian Psychological Services
Roseville Professional Center #435
2233 N. Hamline
St. Paul, Minnesota, 55113
(612) 633–5290

Contents

A study guide to accompany this book
for group or individual study is also available.

Introduction

It's frightening to undertake a book on self-control, and I want to share my misgivings at the very outset. I fear that the reader will interpret self-control as self-generated effort. If we proceed that way, we quickly abandon the only right ground: the grace of God.

Perhaps the best way to show what I mean is with a story.

ERNIE'S PILGRIMAGE

I might have trouble describing Ernie.[1] When I met him at a Bible study meeting, he appeared—well—ordinary. As I now try to recall his appearance, nothing stands out. He was about thirty-eight, of average height and average complexion. He belonged to an average denomina-

[1]Ernie was not his real name. As in the other personal histories recounted in this book, Ernie's story has been altered beyond recognition. Most case examples are the combined records of several persons. Details have been changed. Genders have frequently been switched, occupations masked, locations misidentified. Nevertheless, true-to-life stories have been created. In this way there is no chance of violating anyone's confidentiality—a cardinal sin for counselors. I emphasize this so readers will not assume that with a bit of diligence they can identify the persons referred to. There is no way to do that. Any apparent resemblance to real persons is completely accidental.

tional church attended by average, middle-class people. Ernie installed and repaired refrigeration units, if I remember right. He was married, had some children, and lived in the middle of the middle class.

After the meeting, we went out together for coffee. I had become interested because of certain contributions Ernie had made to our class discussion and, at my request, he told me the story of his own religious pilgrimage. He had nearly given up his faith in despair at one time.

As I said, Ernie went to church. But he'd seldom thought much about God. Then Ernie's pastor preached a series of stirring sermons on renewal, and Ernie was touched by the Spirit of God. He committed his life to Jesus Christ. He asked God to fill him with the Holy Spirit, and his prayer was answered. His life was renewed, never to be the same again. Moreover, Ernie *felt* renewed.

All sorts of wonderful events happened in quick succession. For the first time in his life, Ernie was able to *feel* the presence of God. He began to read the Bible—not as a painful duty, but as a delight. He read as a starving man might consume a banquet. Ernie joined a prayer group that met in his pastor's home. He never tired of being in the presence of the Lord and His people, so he eagerly anticipated each meeting.

The group began seeking victory over sin through prayer and fasting and—lo!—victory was theirs. In rapid succession, Ernie quit smoking cigarettes and drinking alcohol. He found he did not even desire them, though in the past he'd considered those habits indispensable. Moreover, he had ended his association with a group of friends who had met together for years to play poker. To avoid temptations that might present themselves, Ernie severed his relationship with Lee, his best friend. Lee had not experienced renewal, and he continued to drink, smoke and gamble. Ernie rejoiced in his own personal changes.

But there was more to do. Ernie had always had a bad temper, and now he turned his efforts and his newfound spiritual energy toward purging the angry explosions out of his life. For some reason—a mystery to Ernie—the temper did not go away so easily. Meanwhile, much to the chagrin of his wife, Rose, Ernie came to believe it was his duty to drive sin from his house. So he began to badger Rose, demanding she rid herself of both smoking and drinking. And he told her she ought to get to work on losing weight, too. Ernie kept it up. Rose became resentful. Ernie battered her with Bible passages. His outbursts of temper became more frequent, his rage more intense.

After each explosion, Ernie was racked with guilt and remorse. He became aware of a great gulf between his aspirations for purity and the place at which he had arrived. He knew that, in Christ, he was "dead to sin," but he also found that the *power* of sin was not dead. He thought of himself as a failure. He had burned all his bridges—for this! Despair gripped him.

A Christian friend to whom Rose had poured out the story of their troubles confronted Ernie: "You've been trying to walk with the Lord, Ernie. But your efforts have made you proud and unloving. Unless you do something different, you're going to destroy your relationship with Rose—and maybe her soul—completely."

As the friend talked, Ernie felt the anger building again. After all, who was he to talk? He, too, had some bad habits, and Ernie was tempted to tell him to look to himself. But he swallowed his anger and responded evenly, "I've been trying my best to carry out my commitment to Jesus. I gave Him my life, and now I have to offer Him my best. I need to gain victory over every stronghold of sin. I want to offer Him a victorious Christian life. It *has* been hard lately. I'll take what you have said to heart and I'll try even harder."

Ernie did try harder. But the more he tried the worse things became. In the end, he failed utterly.

And so have many others who, like Ernie, begin with a genuine spiritual reorientation and, before they know it, start tackling their sins in their own strength. Many of us begin in the Spirit, but, like the Galatians, we come under the law. We try to produce righteousness. We try to gain victories, but the victories are won by self. We leave the righteousness of Christ behind and proceed to develop a righteousness of our own. We try to achieve purity by the works of the law.

Ernie sought another meeting with his friend. The friend explained, "Ernie, I used to think I would conquer sin for God. But I found that there's no hope of arriving at God's perfection by struggling for more and more will-power and self-effort."

The friend went on to explain that countless Christians, including Paul, Augustine, and Luther, have found that the righteousness we need is not an attainment of our own, but a free gift, given to us by God on account of the blood of Christ shed on the cross once for all. There is no way to merit this righteousness or to perform in such a way as to earn it. Whenever we try to achieve righteousness through our own strength, we will come under the law. For a time we may deceive ourselves into believing in our own successes, thanking God that we are not as other men are. Eventually, many lose hope under the law's unequivocal condemnation. The best outcome possible is to see our weakness, guilt, and utter helplessness.

"When we come to such a state, the glorious good news that Jesus Christ did everything necessary to make atonement for our sins and to empower us to live and walk so as to please God *apart from our own strength, merits, or works* will set us free from condemnation and guilt. If we take His righteousness as the ground on which we stand before God, we will not fall apart because we can't overcome our sins or gain the victories we hear other people crowing about. For we know that our salvation does not rest in the slightest degree on our own performance, but rather comes to us as the gift of a gracious and loving God who has given us eternal life by grace alone.

"Furthermore," said Ernie's friend, "we can know in advance that the more we try to conquer sin, the more we'll experience the power of sin, pulling us down—until we admit that we are, of ourselves, helpless and trust only in the grace of God for the overcoming of sin, just as we've learned to trust Him alone for forgiveness. God wants to be the only source of our victories!"

Ernie listened intently. When his friend left, Ernie began to sense a peaceful conviction that what he'd heard was true. After that, he took a new approach to the Christian life—the approach of faith. He believed God "and it was counted to him for righteousness." He also believed God for the power to overcome temptation.

I have told you Ernie's story to make a point. The key to Ernie's newfound peace, which he shared with me that evening in the coffee shop, must be the key to all progress in the life of the Spirit: The life in Christ is not a do-it-yourself venture, but a gift of grace; we can receive and live it only by faith—no self-generated righteousness will do.

SOME TOUGH QUESTIONS

So what place can a book on "how to gain self-control" have in a life founded on grace?

Is it legitimate for us to make efforts to conquer bad habits? Can we rightly exhort one another to change our ways? Can we help one another learn to walk the way of obedience? Doesn't all that amount to more legalism? Doesn't a book like this simply suggest more self-effort and self-righteousness?

That is what is frightening about writing a book on how to find self-control. What is to prevent people from so construing everything as to put themselves under the law? How can readers avoid thinking only in terms of self and self-generated resources? The end of that road is, very possibly, despair and even eternal death.

Despite this hazard, the Scriptures contain much instruction in how to change behavior, thoughts and feelings. But it is never suggested in the apostolic writings that the *power* to change comes from the self. Instead, the Word exhorts and instructs the new man, empowered by the Holy Spirit, in how to walk so as to please God.

To the reader, this foundational thought: It is the truth, not self-effort, which sets free. When the truth of God's Word is borne to the heart by the Spirit, we can then profit from instruction about our behavior.

Nothing you achieve through the methods set forth here can contribute a thing toward the total and perfect finished work of Jesus and to the righteousness God gives you for His sake. First, settle firmly for yourself the issue of salvation. Trust only in the merits of Jesus, the substitute, God's own sacrifice complete. Trust Him also for the power to gain control over your behavior, for He died to make that power available to you.

That good news is the truth, which, borne in mind and heart, will set you free from self-righteousness and the scourge of the law—free to obey the directions of the Spirit in the Word. "The fruit of the Spirit is . . . self-control."

William Backus
Forest Lake, Minnesota
Christmas, 1986

ONE

How to Understand Self-Control

As Grant got off the elevator at his floor, he reminded himself of the firm pact he had made: *I* will *make it past the candy machine.*

Walking down the hallway to his office, Grant tried not to notice the chrome and glass monster, its lighted glass panels glowing with lithographed pictures of candy bars—nougat, peanut butter, chocolate! He jingled the coins in his pocket. And, almost before he knew what had happened, Grant was wiping chocolate from his mouth and wadding up an empty wrapper.

Another defeat. Grant was beginning to believe that the machine and its sticky temptations had an almost other-worldly power over him.

And indeed, it is almost spooky how totally beyond control our own actions seem sometimes. "I couldn't help myself," one of my employees told me after she lost her temper and verbally blasted an annoying client. "I just flew off the handle!"

Sometimes, when I'm letting important tasks go undone, I tell myself, "I just can't help putting things off. I know I should do them, but somehow I can't make myself get started." I hear quite frequently from my clients about feelings of powerlessness over their own actions: "I can't quit." "I can't be pure." "I can't get good grades." "I can't lose weight." "I can't say no."

We really believe it when we say, "I can't help it."

But it isn't so. Not literally. We can say truthfully, "I can't help breathing, no matter how hard I try to stop." But we can't accurately deny that God has given us what it takes to control our behavior. Even the person who doesn't know God has the biological equipment necessary to control his outward actions.

Take drinking as an example. The verb "to drink" encompasses action involving use of the muscles of the hand and arm, which contract as the drinker grasps and hoists the glass to the lips. So when a heavy drinker tells me, "I cannot help doing this; I can't control myself," I lose track of the meaning of his language. I know that the muscles he is using are not controlled by the involuntary autonomic nervous system, as is his heart, but by messages he consciously sends from his brain down the spinal cord. His arm has bent and hoisted the glass because he ordered it to do so. What, then, can be the meaning of a phrase such as, "I cannot help drinking now"?

If it were a twitch of his eyelid about which he made the statement, I could agree fully. You don't decide to twitch. It's an automatic reflex, usually brought on by fatigue or tension. But bending your arm isn't. That's a decision. Even so, most people have learned to tell themselves that they cannot help doing certain actions—and these actions aren't twitches. They involve the voluntary muscles, muscles that require a decision from the brain before they will perform their tasks.

There seems to be no alternative but to conclude that we must label most of the "I can'ts" and "I have tos" as untruths. It isn't factual to say that we can't help ourselves. But it certainly prevents the exercise of self-control.

THE "I-WANT-IT-AND-I-WANT-IT-NOW" CULTURE

Why is self-control so difficult?

One of the most cogent biblical discussions of the problem appears in Romans 7. Although interpreters have not agreed on whether Paul is writing of his experience before or after coming to Christ, they are agreed that he traces the problem of self-control to the power of sin. To the extent that the sin power remains active in our thoughts and actions, we, like Paul, will have a hard time controlling some of our own behavior.

How does this power manage and control our behavior so mightily? One way is by convincing us that the lies of the devil are true, so that we repeat these false beliefs over and over to ourselves.

Today, every person in the western world (and much of the third world as well) is exposed forcefully and repeatedly to the message that restraint is neither necessary nor good. On the contrary, say our mass media, we will miss many important things in life unless we learn how to let impulses, emotions, and desires have free reign.

An excellent example is the Pioneer Stereo ad which appeared in *Time* magazine with this text; "I was traveling through Europe, when I met this Swedish woman in Malmo. . . . She always used to tell me, 'It's not so important how other people choose to live their lives. If it feels right to you, do it. Just make sure you do it well!' . . . She taught me to enjoy things I never knew existed. And for that, I will always be grateful."*

Some of the axioms we pick up from our media declare that our primary *duty* is "to enjoy"; the world is our "oyster." We simply assume that bad feelings don't belong in a normal life. Pain isn't merely unpleasant, it's made to seem a violation of the rules. We are taught to believe that nobody should suffer, or endure anything unpleasant, or wait for any little thing we might want.

We learn to demand "what we want, when we want it"—to want it *now*!

---

*This is a copyrighted ad of Pioneer Electronics (USA) Inc., appearing in *Time*, November 11, 1985, page 85.

During many initial interviews, I've heard this pathetic type of response: "I am here to get over feeling so bad, Doctor, and I really want to get this taken care of quickly. Can you fix me up? And how long will it take? Really? You don't know? I don't understand, Doctor. Surely you've seen others with the same problem."

People seeking psychotherapeutic help today typically expect to be fixed and fixed fast. Most of them have never once thought that their misery might result from habits of living, believing, and thinking which they have cultivated for a lifetime, and of which they are ignorant for the most part. That they will need to change patterns and alter deep grooves has not even occurred to a majority of them; that there is work and change and pain involved often gets a less-than-enthusiastic, even surly reception. They, too, want instant gratification.

Most of us believe at least some of the prevalent, popular notions about how life should go. To some extent, perhaps, the "I-want-it-and-I-want-it-now" attitude has crept into all of us.

For instance, we may believe firmly that we have a "right to happiness." We confidently expect happiness to be ours right now, free of charge, courtesy of an accommodating God, accommodating parents, accommodating friends, and accommodating scientific and technological breakthroughs—all arranging events so we can get exactly what we want when we want it.

If there is anything wrong, we tell ourselves, it's the result of a breakdown somewhere in the environment, past or present. Our distresses and flaws are "scars" inflicted on us by God, parents, or associates.

We suspect that inhibitions are bad for us, and assume that guilt feelings are harmful. Many think loneliness is just plain evil, conscience pangs are symptoms of psychological illness, and they're maladjusted if fear of God keeps them from doing something they'd enjoy.

Even Christian heads can be saturated with such beliefs as these: Nobody should have to work at paying attention; studies should be made so interesting they involve you without effort; religious teaching should always be exciting, so there's no need to grapple with difficult or intricate doctrines; your daily work should be fascinating and always agreeable; home should always be entertaining; effort is bad. If beliefs like these truly do saturate the intellectual air we all breathe, then we might be expected to have special difficulties with self-control.

THE FRUIT OF THE FLESH IS "NO CONTROL"

In Leningrad there is a magnificent equestrian statue of Peter the Great, with his hand uplifted, pointing his country onward. In many respects, this "Czar of All the Russias" merited the title "Great." But he was subject to fits of rage and, in one of these outbursts, he killed his own son. Toward the end of his life, Peter the Great said, "I have conquered an empire, but I was not able to conquer myself."

Most of us are not quite so bereft of self-control as Peter the Great. We lose our tempers, keep on smoking cigarettes, weaken when someone offers another helping of caramel custard, and let our garages stay messy for too long before we clean up. We don't kill anybody. Our own control deficits fall into more ordinary categories.

Perhaps you've already considered your own need to grow in self-control in specific behavioral domains. For a long time, you've felt as though your eating or drinking or smoking or temper were controlling you instead of vice versa.

Some people find it helpful to use a simple device to spotlight areas wherein they need self-control. The following is a checklist containing a number of common problems related to lack of self-control. There are others. Study it thoughtfully. You may want to check the problems you've noticed in yourself:

__ overeating
__ drinking too much
__ drug abuse
__ binge eating
__ bulimia __ anorexia
__ compulsive washing, cleaning, counting, or check-
ing
__ procrastination
__ being late most of the time
__ TV addiction
__ failure to keep promises
__ wasting time
__ financial problems, credit-card problems, too many
debts
__ sexual compulsions, dwelling on illicit sexual
thoughts
__ smoking
__ temper outbursts, chronic anger, bad disposition
__ inability to say no, "weak will"
__ annoying habits (nail biting, for example)
__ messy closets, drawers, desk top, rooms
__ tasks you never get around to
__ moods and emotions running your life
__ inability to
__ pray and read the Bible regularly
__ get out of bed on time
__ handle suffering
__ exercise regularly
__ get out and meet people
__ study
__ stick to resolutions
__ complete work on time

A MATTER OF MOTIVE

We Christians have a powerful motivation, generated
within us by the Holy Spirit: We want to obey God, to

serve Him, and to please Him. It is this motive that the non-Christian cannot know; it also gives the Christian who is trying to gain control of his life a distinct advantage. Only the Christian has had the deepest desires of his being changed by the power of the Holy Spirit.

The conscience of the new person in Christ Jesus says, "I want to learn self-control in order to live in obedience to Him who loved me and gave himself for me. I know that self-control is the fruit of the Spirit, and that if I'm to attain Christian maturity, I must gain control over my actions and my heart." The aim of the Christian life, therefore, is not to provide oneself with happiness, but to obey God and grow to the maturity He wills for us.

Nevertheless, happiness is a good gift from God. While it is not the end and aim of Christian existence, it comes as a wonderful by-product of the self-controlled life. Although it is a mistake to try to live for happiness as the goal of life (for then happiness becomes a god), it is not wrong to want happiness, especially when it's understood that *happiness comes as a result of wholehearted obedience to God.* Happiness results from an obedient walk with God in *His* way.

THE PARABLE OF TWO STUDENTS

Psychologist Paul Hauck has used the example of two students to illustrate the importance of self-control in finding happiness and success. Both students, when we catch a glimpse of them, are facing final examinations.

One of them thinks, *Studying for finals is too much work. It's boring, dull. I can't see putting myself through all that agony to learn a bunch of stuff I have to know just to please some professor.* So, instead of studying, he goes out to a movie, has a malt and a sandwich, and goes to bed for a good night's sleep.

The other student also thinks how boring and difficult studying for finals will be. But he forces himself to work.

He labors through the professors' notes, learns the textbooks practically from memory, and makes himself sit at his desk until the wee hours of the morning.

Looking in on the behaviors we have described, most observers, says Hauck, would feel terribly sorry for the second student. They would say that he is hard on himself and treating himself badly while the first guy is treating himself very well indeed.

But is that really true? Look at these two students a few months later. The second, the one who put himself through mind-wrenching labor, spends the leisure hours of summer lying on the beach, enjoying the sunshine and the water. The first, the student who took it easy on himself, cannot find time to go to the beach. He is in summer school trying to make up for the failing grades he earned during the last quarter. And so it will go throughout the life of the person who refuses to learn self-control. He will almost always be missing out because he is busy paying for his past mistakes.

LOOK WHO DOESN'T BELIEVE IN SELF-CONTROL

One way to understand how happiness results from learning to control yourself is to look at some people who don't believe it.

The student who had to go to summer school didn't believe it—and brought a summer of unhappiness upon himself.

Steve, a 30-year-old, unmarried engineer is another example. He lived to have sex with as many women as possible. When he contracted an incurable venereal disease, he became angry at the government for not spending more money to discover a cure.

Roger, a salesman who couldn't get himself to make calls on prospects, grew to despise himself because of what he referred to as "laziness." He became so miserable he sought treatment for his depression.

Tania, a cocktail waitress, found herself in bed with a different man every night. Tania didn't believe in self-control. Her self-loathing became so anguished, she went home one day and slashed her wrists.

Jason, a pastor who could not make himself call on people; Rachel, an overweight housewife; Herb, now in the midst of his third hospitalization for alcoholism; David, the king of Israel who authorized murder and then mourned a dead child, because he thought a king's fulfillment should be taken for granted, regardless of the cost—all these and many more sufferers have believed that happiness comes from self-gratification, not self-control.

As I listen to the life stories of many who come to the psychology clinic to try to rid themselves of misery, I continue to realize that the reason for much human unhappiness is the failure to develop self-control. Even more basic is a faulty *belief* system.

Look at the story of Duane as an example.

AS A MAN THINKS IN HIS HEART . . .

Duane sat across from me in my office one morning—or perhaps "slumped" would be a better word.

"There is nothing in my life worth getting up for!" he complained. "I get up, go to work, go home, go to bed. It's a never-ending routine. And I don't get anything in life to make it all worthwhile. I don't even have a girl. I just can't see any reason to go on."

I studied him: Duane was 29, single, paunchy. He had been depressed for five years. I asked him, "Why don't you have a girl?"

"Because I don't try, I guess."

"Why not?"

He responded slowly. "Because I can't stand rejection. Look at me. Look at this gut. What girl would go out with a fat slob like me?"

Now, let's step aside and examine what Duane is saying.

At first, his fear of rejection sounds like a legitimate excuse. After all, we understand how unpleasant that is. And the counselor is very likely at this juncture to be lured into an exploration in search of the deep, underlying cause of Duane's fear instead of pressing on with the task at hand—which is to get Duane to do something about his terrible view of himself, perpetuated and fostered by his unwillingness to do anything about his problems.

In fact, Duane's paralysis was the fruit of a number of *misbeliefs*.* He firmly believed and continually told himself that he couldn't stand rejection or anxiety; that getting a girl ought to be easy; that he should have been born handsome; that it was much too hard to lose weight; that he should not have to be uncomfortable or have to work hard for anything.

It never occurred to Duane that success and excellence require doing things one finds difficult—even tackling boring, unpleasant, and frightening tasks. He had to learn that if he wanted to get well, he would need to come to terms with those things.

Duane's chief *misbelief* supports all the rest. He and countless others who present themselves hopefully to psychiatrists and psychologists for "cure" share the same false premise. Here it is:

> *Happiness just happens. I shouldn't have to do anything, work at anything, put up with anything, or suffer anything unpleasant in order to be happy.*

---

*Misbeliefs = beliefs invented by the devil and propagated by the world and the sinful flesh, which people tell themselves over and over again, and because of which they remain miserable and bound to repeat self-defeating, sinful behavior. For a thorough discussion of misbeliefs, see *Telling Yourself the Truth*, by Marie Chapian and William Backus, published by Bethany House Publishers, 1980.

Because of this (and other wrong beliefs), Duane and scores of others fail to develop self-control, or even realize that the lack of it causes their emotional difficulties.

PSYCHOLOGISTS RESEARCH HAPPINESS

Dr. Michael W. Fordyce is a psychologist who found fourteen characteristics of people who are happy. Here are the fourteen fundamentals as Fordyce presents them:

1. Be more active and keep busy.
2. Spend more time socializing.
3. Be productive at meaningful work.
4. Get better organized and plan things out.
5. Stop worrying.
6. Lower your expectations and aspirations.
7. Develop positive, optimistic thinking.
8. Get present-oriented.
9. Work on a healthy personality.
10. Develop an outgoing, social personality.
11. Be yourself.
12. Eliminate negative feelings and problems.
13. Develop close relationships, the #1 source of happiness.
14. Value happiness.[1]

Of course, there is nothing exclusively Christian about these traits. Nor are Christians the only people who are happy. Furthermore, I want to repeat that happiness is not the aim of the Christian life. The object of Christian living is serving God. However, the Christian Way offers something no other way of life can give: the power of God at work to change behavior.

The non-Christian must change his behavior himself if he is going to change it at all. Not only does a Christian

---

[1]Dr. Michael W. Fordyce, *The Psychology of Happiness* (Cypress Lake Media, 1981).

have the *motive* to change, but he can apply to the heavenly Father for the power of the Holy Spirit—and that gift is never refused. God wills to forgive us our failures in self-control, and to give us new resources to gain control over our behavior in all areas.

Look again at Fordyce's list in this light. For the person who has entered a living, personal relationship with God through Jesus Christ, there are real raw materials for happiness available to no one else. God calls him to a life of active service (point 1); he enters a large fellowship of brothers and sisters with whom he can socialize (point 2); the call of God gives real meaning to his work (point 3); he walks close to God who loves order (point 4); he has Someone who will take all his anxieties (point 5); he is given clear and realistic expectations in the promises of God (point 6); he has, of all men, the best basis for positive thinking about everything because God is in charge (point 7); he can put the past behind because it is forgiven and leave the future up to God (point 8); the Holy Spirit works in him the ability to truly love others (points 9 & 10); he has a new self with which he is enabled to live a truly renewed life (point 11); he has a real answer to problems and the sources of negative feelings (point 12); he has one close relationship with Jesus Christ which remains no matter what happens, and from it he can learn to be close to others, too (point 13); he has a reason to value happiness and contentment because God wills these things for him (point 14).

It is clear to me as I study psychology that though psychologists may be able to describe the characteristics of happy people, they have little to offer human beings in the way of power to change radically and from the heart!

Because Christians can change through repentance and faith in Christ, Fordyce's fourteen points make the most sense to the person who has a vital personal relationship with Jesus Christ together with the gifts and guarantees that go with having God as Father.

Please notice that carrying out such a fourteen-point program for happiness requires *self-control*. Observe that, according to Fordyce, you can't attain happiness by sitting in a corner and telling yourself you can't help your bad habits and you certainly can't tackle all those threatening new situations that seem to position themselves between you and the fulfillment of your dreams. You must carry out a sustained, disciplined program of behavior change if you wish to be happy.

SELF-CONTROL, SELF-IMAGE, AND BEING HAPPY

Often, the very people who need to improve their self-control skills do not attempt to do so because they see little value in self-control. It sounds like a lot of work to them. They are so convinced that what they need in life must come *to* them from the beneficence of others, it never occurs to them that they have been so designed by the Creator as to be unable to live well and happily without learning to use their wills to control their own actions. These same people often have problems with their self-concepts. In fact, in my experience, most people who come to a counselor for help complain that a good part of their misery is due to a poor self-image which they haven't been able to improve.

WHEN YOU DEBATE, SELF-IMAGE ESCALATES

Tell a friend you've got a terrible self-image, and the chances are your friend will tell you what a wonderful person you really are and that you should stop thinking so poorly of yourself. And since it generally feels good to hear positive things from others, you may feel better for a few minutes. But on the whole, this treatment won't help. It never does.

Why not? Let me explain.

People, perhaps unlike animals, don't merely behave

in certain ways. We observe ourselves behaving, note what we do or don't do, *and evaluate ourselves accordingly.* When a person, consciously or unconsciously, sees himself as a goof-off, a failure, all talk and no action, a slave of his feelings, moods, passions, fears, or inertias, he evaluates himself. And his self-evaluation is quite naturally poor. From the point of view of the spiritual objective of self-control, his observations *might even be right.* His track record in one or more areas might be downright bad. That, of course, doesn't mean that he is a worthless person—but he may tell himself it does. Hence, the ugly self-image.

This explains, too, why those who learn to debate the lies and misbeliefs which keep them from changing their behavior patterns almost always notice that they've received a terrific bonus. They discover that they like themselves. Their self-image has changed for the better. In other words, while they debated their inner untruths, they won over the erroneous beliefs which had robbed them of self-control—*and* they saw victories and successes they had never even been close to. Automatically they stopped seeing themselves as losers and failures because they had stopped perpetually losing and failing.

Perhaps you think little of yourself because you learned it from a critical parent or teacher. Nevertheless, you can learn to think more of yourself by becoming master (under the Master) of yourself instead of the helpless slave of your own mental and spiritual juices. You don't think much of yourself now? Imagine how you would feel about yourself if you could look in the mirror and see the person you would like to be!

Imagine the person in your mirror reads his Bible every day and spends quality time with Jesus in prayer, eats and drinks only what he really wants to and in quantities he knows will keep him trim, enjoys aerobic exercise regularly, finishes what he starts, does what he must without procrastinating, cares about the needs of others, makes friends with skill and keeps them by controlling his own interpersonal behavior instead of subjecting others to his moods. You would think a good deal more of yourself if you actually saw that person in your own mirror, wouldn't you? Such an improved self-image is the bonus you can have for developing self-control.

So, although the major reason why Christians want to develop self-control is that they need it to obey and please God, you shouldn't look at this gift as a rather grim habit of never enjoying anything. No, indeed! One strong incentive for self-control is this bonus: You can be happier with yourself than you ever believed possible.

If you believe, now, that self-control is the key to obedience and happiness, you are ready to learn how you can develop it with the direction and guidance of the Holy Spirit.

TWO

How God Gives Self-Control

According to St. Paul, God gives self-control. "The fruit of the Spirit is . . . self-control" (Gal. 5:22). How does God's Spirit bear this fruit in us? In *whom* is it borne?

Everybody develops a measure of self-control, because without some control over our wishes, drives, and appetites, we couldn't live in society. But the spiritual fruit of self-control is something more, and God does not give it to everyone, though His Word declares that He would like nothing better. But this special power to direct our own thoughts, feelings and actions comes as a beautiful gift to those who accept Jesus Christ as their Savior and Lord. On them, God bestows His Holy Spirit who dwells within them and works His marvelous gifts into their being.

Nor does Scripture say that God gives total and perfect self-control immediately to one who receives the Holy Spirit. Paul's readers, for example, who had received the Holy Spirit, demonstrated very little self-control in certain behaviors. Who couldn't use some improvement in self-control over runaway emotions, ugly moods, pernicious habits, or defeating inertia?

33

THE GIFT OF "INSTANT" SELF-CONTROL

Some people receive *instant* self-control over certain behaviors. Once, in a marvelous answer to prayer, I was released on-the-spot from every trace of the desire to smoke tobacco—a habit in which I'd been trapped for twenty-five years. I'd never succeeded in extricating myself, despite numerous attempts to quit smoking. I was also given at the same moment, with no effort whatever, utter freedom from alcohol, which had been much too important and destructive in my life. Others have experienced similar release from life-dominating habits at the hand of God.

But God did not in that same instant give me painless, effortless success in controlling everything. Other domains of behavior remained difficult to gain control over. Results came much more slowly. I don't know why God didn't bestow instant and total self-control in all areas, but He didn't.

In fact, after working with hundreds of fellow Christians to help them gain control over behaviors which were controlling them, after hearing their stories and carefully gathering the facts, I have concluded that God often works in just this way: He bestows self-control instantly in answer to prayer in a few areas, but deals with many other self-control problems by deliberately enlisting us in a daily struggle.

God purposely steers us into battles we *can* lose (though our ultimate victory is His responsibility), shows us where the weapons and armor are kept, and then allows us to try our mettle, never leaving nor forsaking us, but not stepping in to take over the conflict *for* us.

I don't know all the reasons why God gives self-control in this piecemeal fashion, of course. But it seems characteristic of His training program for His people that He makes them develop certain skills through actual practice. We are part of an army, and all armies must learn to win by fighting. There wouldn't be much use for an army if it could do no more than sit around and enjoy miraculous victories.

Any gain we achieve in self-control is a gift from God. Even when our own battle skills and our best efforts are involved, Christian self-control is the creation of the Spirit of God in us. The efforts we make and the skills we acquire were devised and ordered by God in His perfect love.

WHAT SELF-CONTROL IS NOT

Most Christians pray for self-control at one time or another. Maybe you think you need self-control only when you're going to the dentist and you know it'll hurt.

Jess, a bleary-eyed business executive, told me he'd been praying for the gift of self-control to stop drinking martinis at lunch.

I asked him, "How do you picture this gift of self-control?"

He frowned as he thought about it. Then he broke into a grin. "I guess I think of God like a filling station attendant, pumping some fluid labeled 'self-control' into my tank!"

Kris, an overweight co-ed, had a similar idea. She had enlisted my aid in her battle with her waistline. "I'm all right until they pass the candy," she told me. "When that happens, I say something inane like, 'I don't have much willpower.' Then I help myself to another piece of fudge."

Kris imagined willpower as a chunk of something inside her head. Her portion was minuscule, she thought, while some people had giant-size hunks of this power inside. For these people, it was bound to be easy to stay slim, according to Kris. She herself, having been shortchanged in respect to this stuff (whatever it was), could not expect to be able to control herself when it came to eating fudge.

Whether you call it willpower, self-discipline, or self-control, this desirable prize is not a substance like gaso-line that a person either has or doesn't have in his "tank." It isn't a blob of brain tissue large in some fortunate peo-ple, small in others.

"Self-control" is not a *thing* at all. It is the name we give to a class of behaviors. We acquire these behaviors by learning, just as we acquire golf skills, or jumping rope, or spelling by learning.

What characterizes all self-control is the ability to ex-ercise restraint over your thoughts, feelings, desires, and actions so as to achieve your long-term goals. The self-controlled person maintains progress toward a goal *even when he is not in the mood, doesn't feel like making the effort, would momentarily enjoy something else, or finds working toward his goal downright unpleasant.* Instead of doing what comes easily at the moment, he fixes his eye on the long-term goal and works for it, rather than acting on impulse, whim and old habit. The Christian, exercising self-control, makes choices on the basis of his real de-sires—those new desires planted within by the Holy Spirit.

Doing what you have to do instead of putting it off endlessly, pushing yourself away from the table and say-ing no to tempting snacks, putting tobacco, drugs and al-cohol out of your life, acting on the basis of what is good and right instead of doing whatever you feel like, over-coming chronic anger or temper flareups, making the most of time, taking initiative and making friends—these, and other behaviors we attribute to self-control, are not products of a magic super-stuff produced by a fairy godmother's wand. They are behavioral habits you can gain through a process of learning guided by the Spirit of Truth.

THE FIRST SECRET: BEING CONTROLLED BY THE TRUTH

If we peer deeper into the mystery of self-control, we discover that what keeps a person on target, moving toward his goals, achieving success at what he wants to accomplish, while others are sitting on the sidelines envying him and imagining that he has a bigger blob of willpower than they have—what keeps the self-controlled person self-controlled is what he *tells himself* about the situation.

Look up from this page or close your eyes and tune in on your own thoughts. What sentences are running through your mind? Phrases like, "I wonder if this will work for me," or, "Does this guy, Backus, know what he's talking about?" may express the substance of your thought-stream. Sentences like these are called self-talk, internal monologue, or automatic thoughts.

If you want to know what you are telling yourself, tune in on the stream of thoughts running through your consciousness. If you want to know what you really believe about the meaning of events, stop and pay attention to your internal monologue. There you will find an index to your own notions and convictions.

What I want to get across to you is that if your beliefs as found in your self-talk are a collection of lies, partial untruths and inaccuracies, then you will feel miserable and your actions will be self-defeating. Why? Because your feelings and actions are responses to whatever stimuli are running through your internal monologue. If your self-talk reflects truth, your feelings and actions will be positive and constructive, fulfilling the will of God and the goals of your renewed self. Why? Because feelings and behavior are controlled by the beliefs you repeat to yourself in the always-flowing stream of inner speech.

People with self-control have learned to tell themselves the truth about their goals, motives and actions. They find that the truth frees them from bondage, enabling them to do what they want to do, just as Jesus promised it would (John 8:32–33).

How did Verna do it? Take off all those pounds?

Did Mickey really quit smoking? Old three-pack-a-day, yellow-fingers Mickey? How on earth did he do it after all those years and all those failures?

Kevin wrote a book? You don't say! He always said he'd like to write, that he had a tremendous idea for a book. "But I could never make myself sit down and actually write it," he would confide. "Not enough self-discipline, I guess." How did Kevin make himself actually produce the book he'd only talked about for years?

Mark controls his temper now? Doris keeps her house clean? Sylvia doesn't drink? Arnie stopped eating sugar? Dr. Peters is reading his medical journals? Pastor Lee has been giving his sermons thorough preparation instead of preaching off the top of his head?

Most of us watch others achieve mastery over themselves and mutter, "I'd give anything to know how they do it!"

These people and many others are now learning that freedom from old habits, from moods, from always choosing the easiest route comes as they learn to discover the lies they've been telling themselves about control, and then telling themselves the truth.

"WAIT JUST A MINUTE"

"Wait just a minute," hooted Norman, a Lutheran pastor who was in an audience to which I'd been lecturing on how beliefs affect behavior. "I can think of lots of instances when I act *contrary* to what I believe to be right. Isn't that what happens whenever a Christian sins? How can you say our beliefs control our actions, so that right beliefs will lead to self-control?"

I agreed with him that when a Christian sins, he is acting contrary to rules he believes are true and right. "But people are perfectly capable of believing contradictory things at various times. For instance, right this minute, I believe sincerely it would be wrong to steal. But imagine I'm in a different situation. I am destitute and starving, while someone else is so well-off they wouldn't miss it if I took something very, very small—say, something to eat, or even a small, insignificant amount of money. I can easily imagine letting the devil persuade me that *this time, in this instance, for these special reasons,* it's not so very wrong, or God will understand, or I can get forgiveness later."

"Then," Norman replied, "you're saying we may not hold our beliefs constant. We can believe something sitting in church on Sunday morning and believe something very different in a moment of temptation!"

"Exactly," I confirmed. "It's also true that we can *say* we believe something sincerely, and even *think* we believe it. But when the moment for action comes, our behavior may show we really believe something else, and that deep down we never did actually believe what we said we believed. If I consistently act like the people of the world, you and I would both have reason to conclude that I believe the world's assumptions, *no matter how loudly I insist that I believe the tenets* of Christianity."

I mention Norman's insightful question to initiate a thinking process in you.

Ask yourself what you *really* believe—not only when you're sitting in your chair reading a book, but at the moment of temptation. It's *then* you'll discover the misbeliefs governing your bad behavior. And it's those beliefs— the thoughts in your head at the time you lose control— that you need to replace with the truth.

Jesus implied that for His disciples, truth would be the key to opening the door of any prison (John 8:32–33). Today, men, women and children are trying that key in the locks of their own behavioral prisons and finding that it fits. They can open the doors and walk free.

In the next chapter you will find some concrete examples of how replacing misbeliefs with truth can help you to a new life of self-control.

THREE

Self-Control, Misbeliefs and the Truth

Let's look closely at how truthful self-talk works by examining the case of a client I'll call Kirk.

KIRK'S SELF-CONTROL PROBLEMS

My first look at Kirk made me wonder what could have brought him to seek psychological help. Trim and handsome, with dark wavy hair, Kirk appeared to have everything going for him. I looked at the information form he'd completed: He was 26, employed as a newspaper reporter, working part time on a master's degree in journalism; the brief intelligence estimator test in his file suggested his IQ was in the superior range.

"I don't seem to be able to make myself do what I'm supposed to," Kirk began, looking down at his hands. "I'm blowing it in school, taking incompletes in three classes because I can't make myself write papers. And don't tell me to set goals and make schedules," he added quickly, looking up at me. "I've done all that. It doesn't help. I don't follow through. I'm going down the tubes and I'm desperate."

I was beginning to understand why Kirk's tests had showed he was moderately depressed. He was down on himself for his failure to perform and, as a result, he felt inadequate and hopeless about life. I wondered out loud if Kirk was having difficulty sleeping, one of the most common indicators of clinical depression.

"Every night," he responded. "If I do manage to fall asleep, I wake up in a few hours. Then I lie there and think, 'What's wrong with me, anyway? I don't have what it takes. Other people are doing the assignments. They're progressing through the program. I'm a loser compared with them. I've got to start on those papers tomorrow, no matter what!' Finally, the alarm rings and I have to look another rotten day in the face."

"Sounds like you get yourself so demoralized it's hard to start the day."

"Oh, I drag myself out of bed, get to my desk at the newspaper. But I'm too tired after work and on Saturdays to make myself start writing papers. On top of all that, I feel too depressed even to try."

Kirk didn't conceptualize his problem in terms of self-control. He saw it as some sort of mental block, literally preventing him from moving ahead. Like many people with self-control problems, Kirk had worked himself into a vicious circle. He had let his papers accumulate. Then he became depressed about the seemingly insurmountable mass of work he had left undone. Next, he convinced himself that his depression disabled him so he couldn't tackle his work. This, in turn, caused more depression, which caused him to feel even more paralyzed, which led to more depression. And so it went.

As our interview progressed I learned how Kirk had started creating difficulties for himself by catering to the perfectionistic belief that he had to produce superb papers, the like of which had never been seen before. Every time Kirk sat down to write, he found ideas coming to mind. But, regardless of their real merit, Kirk judged them unsatisfactory. None of them seemed to measure up to the overinflated goals Kirk had set for himself. So he rejected every opening sentence which occurred to him, thus put off starting his papers hoping to come up with more marvelous thoughts. No matter what he thought of, Kirk rejected it, believing he had to come up with something better.

With such an approach, Kirk, like many aspiring writers, rendered himself effectively paralyzed, unable to get started on any of his assignments. Though the block had not yet spread to his journalistic endeavors for the newspaper, Kirk was discouraged enough to look for professional help.

"What do you want to accomplish through counseling?" I asked.

He thought for a moment. "I want to feel better about myself. If I did, I might be able to work at getting my life in order."

Like many patients, Kirk had put the cart before the horse. He wanted to feel better before he took up the tasks he had been letting go. He wanted to *feel* well before he *did* well. I believed, however, his first step was to begin doing what he ought to do before his self-image would improve substantially. As I saw it, his depression and battered self-image were outgrowths of his awareness that he was not doing what God had given him to do.

Secondly, it seemed clear to me that Kirk would have to begin thinking different thoughts—telling himself truth instead of crippling misbeliefs—if he was going to make real changes in behavior. In other words, he would need new mental content—literally, to acquire *a new mind.*

Turning things around, I suggested, would involve the deep, inner turning-around the Bible calls *repentance.* Christians truly turning from an old and sinful behavior pattern to a new and God-pleasing set of actions must literally "get a new mind" (the meaning of the Greek New Testament word for *repent*).

Kirk accepted my suggestion, and we began our work with his prayer of repentance: "I'm sorry, Lord, for my sinful failure to pursue the path of duty. Thank you for your forgiveness, and for empowering me for change with the Holy Spirit. I open myself now to receive the new mind with its new truthful beliefs in the name of Jesus." This prayer of repentance has the effect of orienting a person wholly toward the task of change and releasing the enabling power of the Holy Spirit in his life.

Since the Holy Spirit is, in Jesus' words, the Spirit of Truth, Kirk was now in a position by the Spirit's power to change his old, misbegotten, nonsense-laden self-talk, and to replace it with the new mind—that is, the new, truthful self-talk given by God.

I next explained to Kirk how thoughts influence and cause lack of action. I showed him how his belief that he had to write the perfect paper and that nothing else would be acceptable prevented him from using any of his ideas for getting started. We discussed the possibility that this notion was incorrect. In our first session, I didn't succeed in convincing Kirk that he was *not* bound to produce the world's greatest academic papers, and that his perfectionistic belief was untrue. But he did agree that *if* he could come to believe that he should settle for less impossible standards, he could probably get his work done. At the moment, we'd achieved enough to begin.

I also recommended that he keep a record of his old, trouble-making self-control talk—to "catch it while it's fresh," to write it down at the moment it surfaced, blocking his progress. He was to choose any one of his overdue papers and begin working on it. When he felt blocked, as if he couldn't go on, he was to pay attention to his thoughts, asking himself, *What am I telling myself now?* In this manner, he was to start a thought-journal in which one writes everything he might find in his thoughts. "Are you willing to do that?"

"I don't know," Kirk said, shaking his head. "I don't think I'll be able to write the paper. I haven't even been able to get started."

"I understand," I replied. "Still, I'd like you to make the effort. Get as far as you can, even if it's only entering the library and standing in front of the card catalogue. When you feel you can't make any more progress, start logging your self-talk. Then, next time you come, bring the journal and we'll look at your thoughts together. We want to see exactly what you tell yourself that keeps you from producing your assigned papers."

Kirk agreed to try the experiment.

"ANTI-SELF-CONTROL" MISBELIEFS

When Kirk returned for his next appointment, I further explained how our thoughts affect our actions.

A focal teaching of the Christian religion is that what we *believe* is all important, since it determines our orientation toward Jesus Christ, and thus the kind of Christian life we are going to lead. "We walk by faith (or belief)," writes Paul (2 Cor. 5:7). And Proverbs (23:7) teaches us that "as [a man] thinks in his heart, so is he." Our actions follow from what we believe to be true.

Today, psychologists are also discovering that most, if not all, human feelings and actions are responses, *not directly to environmental events, but to our beliefs about events*. In Kirk's case, his writing block was a direct consequence of certain thoughts in his head. These thoughts represent beliefs he held more or less tenaciously. When he activated those particular beliefs by repeating them over and over to himself, they effectively kept him from doing what he knew he ought to do, and what he really wanted to do.

"In other words, I put off writing my term papers because I believe things that prevent my getting started. Is that your theory?"

"That's what I think, Kirk. And our first task will consist of identifying the beliefs you preach silently to yourself to rob you of self-control," I responded. We have already seen that Kirk approached his work with a set of misbeliefs we have labeled *perfectionism*, telling himself that he had to produce work so fantastic and wonderful that it became literally impossible for him to write anything that measured up. So he didn't write.

When we looked at Kirk's journal, a number of misbeliefs related to his perfectionism revealed themselves. Here is a sample of some of the self-talk with which Kirk habitually indoctrinated himself, helping to produce the "block" which appeared so formidable:

"As long as I don't do my papers, I can't fail— risking failure is too dangerous. I don't dare."

For Kirk, anything he might produce that wasn't ultra-superb was equivalent with failure. And Kirk had spent his life avoiding failure. To him, failure was the worst of all calamities. It wasn't merely that he didn't *want* to fail—*nobody* wants to fail. But most people are willing to risk possible failure in exchange for a chance at success. To Kirk and others who share this misbelief, however, failure is so terrible, *nothing* is valuable enough to make the gamble worthwhile. These people see failure as nearly worse than death.

Later, when we got around to discussing the truth about this issue, I tried to help Kirk examine failure realistically. I purposely confronted him with the worst possible outcome. "Suppose you received, say, a failing grade on a paper. What then?"

"Then I'd be a failure, for sure," he responded without hesitation. "Now I only *suspect* I'm no good. Then I'd know it. I couldn't handle that." His voice was low, desperate, as if it were a foregone conclusion that his real worthlessness would surely come to light.

"Couldn't one bad grade on one paper be an accident? A fluke? A result of one instructor's erroneous judgment?" I prompted.

"I suppose all that's possible, but I never consider such

things. A bad grade would be my own fault. It would show I just don't have what it takes."

"Haven't you written other papers in college? You didn't receive failing grades on all your past efforts, or you couldn't have been admitted to graduate school."

"That's true," he replied thoughtfully. "In the past, I've gotten pretty good grades on my papers. Actually, I've never received anything less than a *B*. But I keep thinking there's a first time for everything."

"All right, suppose you did eventually fail at something. Does it make sense to believe that one *F* could make *you* a failure, while numerous successes apparently don't make you a success, in your view? Isn't that lopsided?" I pressed.

Kirk's frown began to fade. "I never thought of it that way. I guess you're right." He let the trace of a smile play about his lips. "It doesn't make sense to make such a big deal of one failure when I've actually done pretty well if we look at the big picture."

As we discussed it further, Kirk saw that a failure is not a person who fails once in a while to reach some goal he sets for himself. Then I showed Kirk from Jesus' parable of the talents (Matt. 25:14–30) how God defines failure. If you will read this lesson, taught by our Lord, you will learn that, in truth, *a failure is a person who doesn't try*.

So Kirk learned how to tell himself the truth and how to challenge his failure misbelief. "Even if I get an *F* on this paper, and that isn't very likely, in view of my record, it won't make me a failure. The only thing that can make me a failure is not trying."

This was not Kirk's only misbelief, and his treatment involved considerably more work. In due time we had to tackle the perfectionistic misbeliefs with which he'd kept himself miserable for years, among other misbeliefs. He rapidly began work on his papers and completed all of them before the end of the academic quarter.

Perhaps equally important is the fact that Kirk's depression lifted and his self-image ceased to be a concern. With a new set of beliefs—thoughts which elicited effort to produce instead of paralysis—Kirk stopped seeing himself as worthless, and began to feel good about life.

You will encounter some of Kirk's other misbeliefs in future chapters. Our purpose here has been to show how God gives self-control to those who will take the trouble to identify their inhibiting misbeliefs and replace them firmly with spiritual truth, empirical reality and logic.

HOW TO LOCATE YOUR SELF-CONTROL MISBELIEFS AND CHANGE THEM

You will not necessarily discover your own self-control misbeliefs while you're curled up in your favorite chair reading this book. Maybe some of them will occur to you, maybe not. We often hide our own errors from ourselves. If, however, you want to make progress, you will need to work with a method.

Here is what I suggest.

TAKE ISSUES ONE BY ONE

Work on only one self-control behavior at a time. If you're trying to lose weight, stop procrastinating, quit smoking, change your diet, study the Bible regularly and stop having temper explosions all at once, you're not likely to make much progress with any of them. Choose the problem you'd like to handle first. Then, when you have established good control, go on to another.

BEGIN WITH REPENTANCE

Begin with a prayer of repentance. In both the Old and New Testaments, the act of repentance connects people who want to change with the God who gives power for change. In the Old Testament, the Hebrew word for repent is *shuv*. This word means literally turning around (to go in the opposite direction). In the New Testament, the word is *metanoiete*. This Greek imperative means, "Get a new mind!" Believe that God willingly and lovingly erases your sin and guilt for Jesus' sake and by virtue of His atoning blood. Believe that God will, through Christ, not merely forgive your sins, but take them away and replace them with the self-control you need for change.

START A JOURNAL

Start a self-control journal. I suggest you use a pocket-size, spiral-bound notebook you can carry with you. You will use this notebook to record episodes of behavior representing the self-control problem you're working on. You will also use it to record your self-talk, identify your self-control misbeliefs, your efforts to challenge and debate those misbeliefs, and the truth replacing each misbelief as you discover it.

Such a journal will serve as a permanent record to which you can refer back if the problem should arise again. It will enable you to count the frequency with which particularly harmful untruths occur in your self-talk, and thus actually note progress as these misbeliefs return to haunt you less and less frequently. Recording episodes of failure and success in the particular self-control area you are working on will allow you to see concrete evidence of change and improvement.

GET IT WHILE IT'S HOT

Be sure to be aware of the principle of paying attention to your self-talk *at the time of its occurrence*. Get it while it's hot! When you're thinking about something you really ought to start doing, *that is the time* when you can find the misbeliefs causing procrastination in your head.

When you're battling the urge to eat several candy bars is the perfect time to discover what you tell yourself to wreck your weight-control program. Get out your notebook as soon as possible and write those thoughts down. Waiting until later may be too late. It's easy to forget those slip-enabling misbeliefs quickly (especially if it all seems too painful to think about, because we've blown it again). Here is a sample page from Kirk's journal:

Blocking Journal

Feb. 9 — *Episode*: Went to library to begin work on English paper. Sat down to write. Opening sentence came to mind.

Misbeliefs in self-talk: Told myself, "That's trite. You've got to do better than that. Any fifth grader could come up with a more original opener. You don't have what it takes, Dummy."

Debate and Truth: "Why do I have to come up with a better opener? This one may not be the most brilliant first sentence ever, but it will do. I can write it down for now. If I want to, I can change it later on when I write another draft. For now, what counts is to get something on paper—anything will serve the purpose for this first draft."

Result: Actually began writing, completed 3 pages. Plan to revise and rewrite later.

OTHER TACTICS

The most common mistake made by writers of books on self-improvement is to give the impression that we are telling the whole story when we recount a portion of a true-to-life case history. Most often, we are telling you a shortened excerpt from a much longer story.

Readers could go over the above brief account of a portion of Kirk's treatment and get the impression that it's an instant cure. As a matter-of-fact, we had to continue to work quite hard, over a period of months to achieve Kirk's goals.

We are all on the lookout for easy answers. We are suckers for the charlatan who tells us, "All you have to do is . . ." and then provides a quick and easy formula for success. Reality, even with an effective counseling method, rarely offers quick and easy solutions to problems.

I know that the crucial events which must take place if a person is to recover from a psychological "ailment" boil down to replacing inner untruths and misperceptions with the truth: I also believe there are a number of ways to get there. A person can develop self-control by learning to tell himself the truth in place of the collection of false beliefs that keep him at the mercy of his own whims. But there may be more than one way for him to learn to do this and to actually put it into practice. Treatment may require the use of several tactics.

In Kirk's case, we did more than debate his misbeliefs. We worked at uncovering and facing squarely some of the traumatic events in his history through which he learned his erroneous convictions about performance and failure. We prayed that the Holy Spirit would implant the truth in Kirk's spirit. We made schedules, kept records of Kirk's improving performance, and planned for Kirk to reinforce himself for small gains. We kept our eyes on the truth as a goal, and used various strategies to help us to discover and/or implement the truth in Kirk's life.

In this book, you will find that I suggest a core strategy: using a journal to locate, identify, challenge, and replace a variety of beliefs with the truth. I will also offer additional tactics you can employ to improve self-control in succeeding chapters.

Whatever the specific strategy suggested, I believe all of them are ways of replacing the misbeliefs in our self-talk with the truth God has built into His creation and His Word.

FOUR

How to Stop Putting It Off till Tomorrow

"I wish I could make myself balance my checkbook every month. If I did, my bank account wouldn't be in such chaos. Why do I always avoid that job until financial disaster threatens?"

"I can't seem to get going and get things done when I know I ought to do them. I tell myself, 'I'm going to start reading the Bible every day.' But that's as far as it goes. I can't even get myself to begin. What's wrong with me?"

"I've been promising my wife I'll clean the garage next Saturday for six or eight months. By the time I got around to waxing our new car, it was too late. The finish had already taken a terrible beating."

"I really ought to make an appointment with the dentist. It's been three years since my last visit."

"I feel so guilty. I promised to call Marian. But I've put it off so long I'm embarrassed to even talk to her."

Do these phrases sound familiar? Do you go around in pain from chronic, nagging guilt because you needlessly put off doing what you know you ought to do? Complaints like these sometimes surface in the psychologist's consulting room. More often, people with such complaints put off getting help or making efforts to change.

Does everybody procrastinate?

Yes, in some way. Procrastination is putting things off instead of doing them when they should be done. Most people are careful not to postpone when the consequences would cause disaster. Once in a while, however, nearly everyone gets into trouble by letting something slide.

Some more serious procrastination habits are chronically harmful, deeply-rooted, and resistant to change. Such habits can rob us of God's best blessings.

FAVORITE THINGS WE PUT OFF

Which of these do you put off until you have real problems? Think about it:

___ returning phone calls
___ doing homework
___ paying bills
___ entertaining
___ balancing checkbook
___ writing papers
___ doing the ironing
___ answering letters
___ going to the dentist
___ cleaning cupboards
___ sending cards
___ visiting new neighbors
___ deciding where to live
___ preparing a speech
___ deciding on a career
___ shopping for Christmas
___ writing thank-you notes
___ returning library books
___ buying gifts
___ going to the doctor
___ planning vacations
___ buying winter clothes

___ deciding what to buy
___ choosing a movie to see
___ starting an exercise program
___ keeping up with exercise
___ going on a diet
___ staying on a diet
___ quitting something (like smoking, eating sugar, drinking coffee, using alcohol)
___ finishing projects you've started
___ Other: _____

Did you notice, when you reviewed the list, how procrastination problems occasionally mesh with other self-control difficulties? That's because people commonly put off starting to work on bad habits, preferring to avoid the unpleasantness and effort they expect to encounter.

You can also observe from the checklist that we tend to procrastinate most with particular kinds of behavior: decision-making and choice-making, for example: starting projects or programs; or finishing what we've begun.

JUST LAZY?

I had seen Judy for eight sessions. We had worked quite successfully to improve her communication skills. I thought we had nearly finished our work together when, suddenly, Judy surprised me during our ninth session.

"I'm just lazy, that's all there is to it," Judy groused, leaning forward in her seat as she had during her very first session weeks before.

Lazy? I thought, mentally reviewing our sessions. I couldn't recall hearing any complaints before about her activity level. Automatically, I checked over her appearance: As always, Judy's grooming was perfect, her clothes were stylish and neat, and every hair was in place. *I doubt that she's lazy,* I concluded. I wondered if she was having difficulties with procrastination.

As Judy explained her outburst about laziness, I saw that *laziness* played no part in her difficulties. The real problem, I learned, was that Judy had a habit of avoiding tasks she didn't feel like doing. As the undone duties piled up, she finally suffered from so much guilt she couldn't live with herself. Then, to give herself a reason why she let things slide, she would tell herself and others how indolent she was.

For instance, her husband complained frequently that he was out of clean shirts. That was when Judy repeated her old refrain: "Oh, I'm such a lazy frump! I don't know how you put up with me!" But she hadn't found time to iron the mound of shirts that spilled out of her laundry basket.

In that session, I asked Judy to log her activities every day until we met. The next week, I found that, in fact, Judy kept very busy. She went to the gym three times a week, attended several classes at church, and put in endless hours working for pro-life causes. Almost never did she sit and do nothing.

Now, with the evidence of her very active life in front of her, Judy had to face the fact that her old cliché about being lazy was just a defense. She was ready to seriously examine her real reasons for putting things off.

Although, like Judy, many procrastinators ascribe their inaction to "laziness," putting things off is seldom caused by a general tendency to do nothing. In fact, if you observe yourself carefully, you may find that you exert enormous effort to put things off—more effort than it would take to do them! Like Judy, you may be maintaining procrastination with excuses. Here are some other rationalizations procrastinators give for their dilatory behavior:

- I'm too busy.
- I have too many things to do.
- I don't know what to do first.
- I don't have time.

- I can't do it well so I won't do it at all.
- I don't know how.
- I'm not in the mood to do anything I find disagreeable.
- I'm too tired.
- I'm sick of doing that.
- It's too trivial to bother with—other things are more important.
- I should do some other things before I start that.

FORGET THE EXCUSES! WHAT'S YOUR REAL REASON FOR DAWDLING?

Once you put aside your excuses, you are ready to face the fact that procrastination is a self-control problem. To conquer it, you will have to look without flinching at your true reasons for letting things go.

Sy was a small businessman, trying to fulfill the dreams of a lifetime, but, alas, he was skirting the edge of ruin because of procrastination.

"I want to find out why I don't keep up with my book work," replied Sy when I asked him his reasons for seeking help. "I'm always on the edge of the cliff with the Internal Revenue Service, and several wholesalers have refused to sell to me—all because I don't keep my accounts in order. Why can't I make myself keep financial records up-to-date?"

Before we look further at Sy's story, it's important here to examine the counseling process. When you ask a counselor *why*, you're liable to get any of several kinds of answers.

Christian counselors, in my experience, frequently look for a *historical* answer. Example: "Sy, it looks as if the reason for all this is the traumatic embarrassment you suffered when your third-grade teacher made fun of your arithmetic paper in front of the class. He so shamed you for the disorderly arrays of numbers on the paper that your inner self is scarred and injured in this area, and to avoid aggravating those old injuries, you still try not to have anything to do with numbers."

Others will come up with a *label*. Example: "Sy, your problem stems from the fact that you are *codependent*. Your entire family shared in the illness of your alcoholic father, and you are still suffering from it. So you hook yourself so tightly to someone else, your ups and downs depend on what the other person does. Therefore you are not your own person and not free to determine your actions for yourself." There are many labels that often pass for reasons and explanations. Usually, however, labels don't explain very much.

A third favorite is a *dynamic* explanation. The behavior is accounted for by variables in the individual's unconscious mind. Example: "Clearly, Sy, you developed a deep *unconscious hatred* for your alcoholic father, together with an *unconscious fear* of competing with him for your mother's affection. Since he was an accountant, your fear and hatred of your father caused you to avoid bookkeeping."

Very commonly, too, Christian counselors explain this and other self-control problems as *demonic bondage*, in league perhaps with *sinful desires* in the old nature. Example: "Sy, a demonic force has your will partially under control to such an extent that you are unable to make yourself do your accounting." In my view, this one is always correct *as far as it goes*, since the ultimate source of evil is the devil, working together with the world and the flesh.

Is there any reason why all four of these explanations should not be facets of the truth? They are not mutually exclusive. They may, in fact, all play some part in generating Sy's problem. Furthermore, the therapist may have to deal with all of them in the process of treatment. In other instances, he won't have to mention any of them in order to change procrastination behavior.

COGNITIVE PSYCHOLOGY

There is one more level of explanation which, according to recent research, may be all that is necessary to lead many people to rapid recovery from numerous psychological maladies. It makes possible brief, effective therapies, and self-help books offering workable tactics for change.

This fourth level is our focus at the moment. It is the reply of *Christian cognitive psychology* to Sy's request for an explanation. Here is an example of such a response from a misbelief therapist: "Sy, you really believe and actively tell yourself that you must do your accounting flawlessly; that you simply can't afford many mistakes; that any error would mean you are stupid and totally inadequate. And you believe that as long as you don't 'get around' to doing your accounting work, you can't make any errors. Therefore it seems crucially important to save your shaky self-image from wounds by *not* doing your accounts."

As you can see for yourself, I trust, these notions are untrue. Because they are lies, they must originate with the father of lies, the devil (John 8:44). Sy, like all Christians, still carries around the flesh even though he is free from its power through Christ Jesus and therefore does not have to submit to it. Sy's old self has bought the devil's line and believes the lies, and Sy repeats them to himself as if they were so. As we discussed earlier, we call his erroneous beliefs, sponsored by the devil and the flesh, *misbeliefs*.

Sy's misbeliefs account well enough for the disastrous postponing of his bookkeeping. He can start working to get well right away. In his case and many others, there is no real need to pursue other levels of explanation. Very likely, you, too, can go directly to the task of finding your own procrastination misbeliefs and learning to challenge and replace them with truth.

SHOOTING DOWN YOUR PROCRASTINATION MISBELIEFS

Many of the misbeliefs in the self-talk of habitual procrastinators are the misbeliefs of perfectionism, of people who think they must reach impossible standards in *every* activity they attempt. Such people feel terribly upset when they believe they aren't doing something superbly. They thus criticize themselves unmercifully, and writhe in agony when they believe others are thinking critical thoughts about them—not to speak of practically dying if someone speaks critically *to* them.

Remember Kirk, the graduate student whose writer's block prevented him from completing his term papers? He discovered that his "block" was actually his misbelief that unless his papers were absolutely stunning, he would have to consider himself a failure, a total washout. Therefore Kirk believed he couldn't afford to take the risk involved in completing a paper.

Kirk's block might be seen as a form of procrastination. Many procrastinators suffer from Kirk's failure misbelief. So we'll list it as #1.

Procrastination misbelief #1: *I must not fail because that would mean I'm a failure. It would be so terrible to fail, it's much better not to try anything.*

Perhaps you are convinced that you might fail if you really worked on the project you've been postponing, and that if you did fail it would prove that *you* are a failure. But what, pray tell, is a *failure* when the term is applied to a person? One who has failed to achieve something he has tried to do? If that's your definition of a failure, everyone is a failure because nobody has achieved every single thing he's ever set his sights on.

Brent was a gifted 17-year-old who had set his sights too high, allowing himself no grace. He was seemingly unable to make himself complete the application process for college. Day after day, he put off filling out and mailing the necessary forms. Meanwhile, he was supporting his procrastination and making himself depressed with the failure misbelief. He told me point blank he was a *failure* and had the evidence to prove it. He had applied for a job in the Washington office of one of his state's two senators. He was turned down. He had fought hard for a tennis championship and lost in the semi-finals. After his application for an appointment to the United States Air Force Academy was rejected, he became so discouraged he labeled himself a *failure*.

"Brent," I responded, "one way to succeed at nearly everything is to try only for easy goals you can reach without question and without risk or effort. By the same token, one way to make failure more likely is to try for high goals that are difficult to attain. You're trying for the best. You can expect more turn-downs and failures than your friends who apply for jobs at fast-food restaurants and for admission to the local junior college."

As I see it, the person who fails most often may be the person who tries for extremely difficult objectives. Or, to put it another way, the person who makes frequent attempts to succeed at various pursuits may experience more frequent failures, too. By contrast, the person who doesn't try at all won't experience any failures. But it would certainly be a misnomer to label such a person a *success*. Is the point clear? The term *failure* when used as a label for a person is meaningless and misleading.

Brent was able to overcome his procrastinating and complete his application. He first learned to challenge his failure misbelief and to tell himself something like this: "Yes, I've failed to achieve some of my goals and succeeded at others. It makes no sense to call myself a *failure* just because I tried to achieve the highest goals. Instead, I can learn from attempts that didn't pay off. In fact, the Lord can often teach me more through those than through my successes. So I refuse to call myself a *failure* and I'm not going to quit trying for difficult goals."

Here are some more misbeliefs frequently held by procrastinators. When you read some of them, you may think, "What's wrong with that one? It's perfectly true!" because you sincerely believe and tell yourself some of these widely endorsed errors. But you will be able to see their flaws and falsehoods as we examine them together.

Procrastination misbelief #2: *There must be one best way to do everything. I won't start anything until I discover the single best way to do it.*

"We never have guests for dinner," said Frieda, "because I don't know how to prepare the kind of fine, gourmet meals one should serve to company." Frieda planned to take a gourmet cooking course someday. Meanwhile, she and Jeff owed everyone they knew invitations to dinner! Jeff was trying to be patient. He couldn't understand why Frieda didn't prepare and serve guests her own good cooking. "He doesn't realize that there is a right way to treat company," Frieda explained, "and I'm the sort of person who needs to do things the best way possible." By hanging on to this absurdity, Frieda effectively persuaded herself to put off having guests indefinitely. Frieda, you must remember, truly believed this hamstringer, and because of it she couldn't get her social life going.

Let's see where her misbelief takes us. Let's imagine that she is right, that there really is only one best way to prepare a dinner. Even if that were so, wouldn't that single best way be understood by only one or two people in the world, master chefs who have excelled everyone else in the art of cooking? Who else could hope to equal them? On the grounds of Frieda's assumptions, *nobody* else should ever have dinner guests, at least until they can be sure they have equalled or excelled the masters!

But is there only one best way to do everything? The truth is that there is usually no single best way to do things, and even if there were, it's absurd to conclude that nobody who isn't "the world's best" should do anything.

Frieda learned to identify and debate against the misbelief that there is only one best way to do anything. She deliberately practiced telling herself something like this: "If I really wait until I find the best way to do everything, I'll do very little indeed! Instead, when I meet a challenge, I'm going to give it a try, do it as well as I can, and realize that God never told me I had to do everything better than my friends. Of course, I'll have to admit once in a while that I could have done something a whole lot better. But as long as I don't tell myself I have to be *best*, I can always try again and perhaps improve."

I can't say that Frieda immediately filled her entertainment calendar with prospective dinner guests. But when I last saw her she had prepared and served company meals three times. Her self-talk logs revealed that frequently during her planning and preparation for these evenings, Frieda had to do battle with the old "one best way" misbelief. And she wasn't always 100 percent comfortable. But she managed to do things she'd never done before. I was confident that with practice, Frieda's discomfort would disappear and, indeed, by the time we terminated it had lost most of its hold.

Procrastination misbelief #3: *It's too hard. Things should be easy. I shouldn't have to do anything that isn't easy. I shouldn't have to exert myself, or be uncomfortable, or do unpleasant tasks. There has to be an easy way to do it, and I won't start until I find it.*

Clancy was hooked on a drug. Not a street drug; it had been duly prescribed for him by a physician—but he'd been taking it for fourteen years! He knew he should break off his love affair with this chemical crutch, but he kept putting off the moment of decision. Clancy frequently had to speak before large audiences. He had discovered that, without the tranquilizer, he *might*, on occasion, become nervous. For him, being nervous meant a pounding heart, rapid breathing, tense muscles and dry mouth. Clancy had convinced himself that these less-than-pleasant events were too much for him to put up with. When he sought treatment to enable him to discontinue the drug, I responded as I often do in similar cases, "There is nothing I can do. Not as long as you believe you shouldn't have to put up with any anxiety. If you want to get over your nervousness, you'll have to be willing—at least temporarily—to go through it."

Clancy looked at the door, as if he were ready to wash his hands of me before we even started. "Can't you hypnotize me or something so I won't feel so nervous?" he asked bitterly. "I could kick the tranquilizer that way. I really should get off these pills, you know. I've had to take more and more over the years. Now I'm taking four or five times as much medicine as my doctor said."

Clancy believed there had to be an easy way to make speeches without feeling nervous, and for years his drug use had fostered that illusion. Because of his firm faith in the error of an easy way, he kept putting off doing anything about his drug problem. When I replied that there was no easy way, but that he could improve if only he would be willing to go through some unpleasantness, he decided not to pursue therapy. I lost him as a patient, but I had the satisfaction of knowing I hadn't strengthened his misbelief that there has to be a painless way to break his drug dependence, and that one should not bother working at it until the easy and comfortable way presents itself.

Clancy's notion that there must be an easy way to do everything is very popular. If God were to take an opinion poll, everyone might vote for it. But wishing doesn't make things so. And, as a moment's thought will make clear, it's not true that there has to be an easy way to do everything, a cheap, painless route through every thicket.

Jesus taught, for example, that following Him might involve quite a bit of sacrifice and discomfort. Though He said, "My yoke is easy," He never tried to portray His way as pleasant and comfortable for the flesh. In fact, He taught that the way to destruction was much less difficult to get on and stay on than the narrow road to Life.

In sports, music, academic pursuits and career (although it occasionally happens that someone gets a lucky break), it is the person who works hard, forces himself to practice when others are fooling around, holds himself to tasks that bore, does not shrink back from activities because they are "hard"—it is *that* person who succeeds. Conversely, the person who is always easy on himself, always chooses the activity demanding the least effort, always takes the path of least resistance, always avoids boring or routine jobs, always passes up genuine opportunities to wait for something easier and more comfortable—*that* person won't get very far in life.

It takes thoughtfulness and effort to be a good friend, to have a happy marriage, or to relate well to your children. It requires painstaking hours of study to learn the Word of God thoroughly. If you want to ride a horse, you'll need to suffer the discomfort of sore muscles and the risk of being thrown. If you desire to play golf, you'll have to put up with the embarrassment of executing some pretty silly-looking shots. There is no reason at all for the widespread belief that things should be easy if you can just wait for the right breaks to come your way. On the contrary, most worthwhile pursuits are difficult, demanding, and attainable only by those who are willing to put up with considerable boredom, discomfort and frustration.

Unless you have a written contract in your pocket signed by God, it's ridiculous to claim that you should be exempt from the difficulties ordinarily faced by most of the human race, meanwhile putting off getting to work until some simple, obvious, effortless route toward the goal shows itself to you.

> **Procrastination misbelief #4:** *Anything worth doing is worth doing well, and that means I must do it perfectly. A flaw in my performance makes it terrible and worthless and indicates that I'm no good. I should always wait for the perfect option before I make a decision.*

"I'm just a flop!" Thora announced to her roommate, Betsy, as she slammed the front door. Betsy knew from experience what was bugging her friend. Thora had spent the evening with Warren—and Warren had proposed again. He loved Thora, who was also deeply in love with him. But somehow she couldn't bring herself to make the critical decision. Whenever she felt close to giving her consent to marriage, a little voice in her head would whisper, "He doesn't know you well enough. Just wait. When he discovers what you're really like, he won't want you. What if that happened after you were married? You can't say yes now. You have to be perfect first. Don't make a decision now. It might be the wrong one!"

Thora's learning history had filled her with erroneous ideas. She believed she must never choose any option unless it was perfect—so she rarely made choices. Decisions were, as she put it, "murder" for her. She always tried to put them off indefinitely. And she knew that she herself had faults. She was pretty successful in her efforts to hide her faults from everyone except God. But Thora knew that in a really close relationship, her foibles would come out. Then, as she saw it, she would stand unmasked, revealed as a worthless creature. For, by Thora's creed, any little blemish meant no one could possibly want her. No sensible person who knew what she was really like would marry her.

Betsy tried to tell Thora she didn't have to be perfect to marry Warren, but Thora wouldn't let go of her misbeliefs. She wouldn't let go of Warren either. She just kept stalling, procrastinating, refusing to make a decision, until at last Warren, in frustration, ended their relationship.

It simply isn't *so* that anything worth doing is worth doing well. Some things are worth doing, but only in a sketchy manner. Often it is much better, for example, to skim a newspaper than to spend two hours reading it thoroughly. You would be foolish to polish your grammar and resort to a Thesaurus if you're only ordering a pair of boots from Sears. Should you skip eating if you aren't in the mood to work hard on a seven-course dinner? A flaw means only that you are human and that you are still alive. The flawless have already gone to heaven. Far from concluding that there is something terrible about you, that you are a dud or a failure, when others discover imperfections in you, they are apt to conclude only that you are human. Nobody wants another person who puts up a front, especially a front of perfection.

You cannot have a close relationship without revealing your faults. Had Thora revealed herself, even her flaws, without so much anxiety, to Warren, she might have developed a valuable, close relationship with him and might even have shared with him a happy marriage. Waiting for perfection often means waiting forever. Delaying decisions until the perfect option presents itself results in circumstances making decisions for you.

> **Procrastination misbelief #5:** *I must never, never, never make a mistake.*

Ned was a middle-aged pastor serving a thriving suburban church. Muscular and good-looking, with graying hair and a warm, resonant voice, Ned projected an image which both attracted people and gave them confidence. Ned labored to do all his tasks faultlessly. He was caught up in pleasing others, in keeping the goodwill of the members of his flock. He tried to do everything, be everywhere. He preached three different sermons every Sunday, and another on Wednesday nights. He attended all the committee meetings, appeared at all social events, and made himself available during the Saturday night youth gatherings in the church basement. Ned never refused to see anyone immediately, or as soon as he could free himself from whatever else he was doing. And he made precisely five pastoral calls every day except Sunday. When he could get a few hours to himself, Ned studied theological materials and all the psychology he could get his hands on. He spent a minimum of four hours' preparation for each sermon he delivered. He couldn't stand it if he thought he had made a mistake for which someone might criticize him. He lived in fear of saying something wrong, or of giving someone the wrong impression. He would pray fervently, "O Lord, help me to do my work so that no one finds fault with me and therefore with you." He never noticed that God puts His treasure in earthen vessels so the treasure will show up brighter by contrast.

Ned's approach to his work created enormous strain which took its toll. Eventually, Ned's fear of making a mistake became so intense he could no longer force himself to work on his sermons. He began to deliver them extemporaneously. No amount of resolve kept him from putting off preparing—until it was time to step into the pulpit and there was no further possibility of postponement. Ned's anxiety mounted. He told himself he was failing—failing to prepare conscientiously, failing to handle his anxiety, and therefore failing as a Christian. He was sure his feelings would show and he would be found out. He believed he would be unmasked and roundly criticized for his weakness, scorned for his failures. Eventually, Ned resigned his ministry, defeated by his own misbeliefs.

Mistakes are seldom fatal. Yet, numerous people like Ned drive themselves to the point of collapse to try to avoid making mistakes. It isn't simply that they would rather do things right than make errors. No, it's more than that. They believe that mistakes are unforgivable, worse than death, and that they must be avoided no matter what toll they take on the human system. One year, I was given a chess set for Christmas. But this chess set is a computer. And it plays against me at whatever level of difficulty I choose. It is nearly impossible for me to win against this machine. And do you know why? It *never* makes a mistake. It can be relied on *never* to move a piece into danger of capture unless it can gain an advantage by so doing. It has no bad days, no lapses of memory, no overlooked opportunities. All because it is a computer, a machine. You are not a machine. You're a person. And persons, ever so much better designed than computers, make mistakes, nevertheless.

Ned believed that, were he to make a mistake, it would totally destroy him and his ministry. Do you believe, with Ned, that mistakes are so terrible you can't allow yourself to do anything at which you might make one?

As a matter-of-fact, mistakes are rarely terrible. Often, they can be positive events, evidence that you haven't been content to fall back on your old achievements, but that you are willing to work at tasks you have not yet become good at. Even if you make the same mistake over and over again, it is absurd to use this as evidence that you are no good, a total loss, or a stupid bumbler. Most often, such things mean merely that you need further instruction or more practice. This misbelief, like the others, can drown you in inactivity if you really live out its implications, because it can ultimately keep you from trying anything.

OTHER NONSENSICAL NOTIONS REPLACED BY THE TRUTH

There are other nonsensical notions which can result in procrastination. Here are a few more misbeliefs procrastinators sometimes find lurking behind their stalling. You may discover some of them when you investigate your internal procrastination monologue.

> **Procrastination misbelief #6:** *It's too much work. I'm too tired. I don't have the energy to do it. Maybe I'll feel more rested later.*

What do you mean when you say something is "too much work"? Literally, the expression means that the energy you would have to expend doing something would be such a great amount you would collapse, unable to move, before you could finish. Only a person devastated by physical illness or extreme age would really and truly "not have enough energy" to complete ordinary tasks. It might not be as pleasant to do your work when you are tired or listless, but it's almost never impossible. Telling yourself that something is too much work only supports procrastination.

> **Procrastination misbelief #7:** *Someone else is better at this. If I do it, I'll show that I'm not as good. I can't stand being second. So I can't do it.*

Why can't you stand being second? Will you die if you are second-best at something? Or lose the love of your family and friends? Or take a big cut in income? No? You mean only that you don't like being second? But isn't it nearly always true that someone else is better at the pursuit than you? Even if you play the oboe superbly, someone, somewhere is better. If you are a great star at volleyball, someone in some nation in the world, can outdo you. Perhaps you have been praised for your writing. But there are likely many who are better writers than you. Only a very few human beings in the world can be first at anything, and even they have to accept being second in most endeavors.

> **Procrastination misbelief #8:** *There is a perfect time to do everything and this is not it. I can't do a task until the perfect moment for starting it arrives.*

What's really wrong with *now*? Often there is no better time to do things you tend to put off. I have discovered that it is often best to do things I'd rather put off *now*—then later, as a reward for completing the disagreeable task, do the things I would rather do because I enjoy them. There is, of course, no perfect time to do most things. Nearly every activity can be pursued at any number of times or occasions, so there is no perfect moment and no sense waiting for it. If *now* really isn't a good time, then plan for the right time and do the things you are putting off.

> **Procrastination misbelief #9:** *I can't start this because I have to do something else first.*

This one is sometimes reasonable and true, but more

often it's a device for avoiding and putting off something you know you ought to tackle.

Often procrastinators keep themselves terribly busy at routine tasks such as cleaning and straightening up the desk top, filing papers, or rearranging books. None of these things really *have* to be finished now. Generally, the consequences of postponing desk straightening are slight, while the consequences of postponing pressing and important tasks *in order to straighten the desk* are likely to be more serious. We should always challenge this procrastination misbelief, asking ourselves precisely *why* it's important to do something else first.

> **Procrastination misbelief #10:** *Somebody will surely criticize and pick it apart, and I can't stand that, so I can't do it.*

Has your work ever been criticized in the past? Did you stand it? You didn't like it, of course, but you *did* stand it, didn't you? You got through it. You didn't die from it. You found it unpleasant. Unless you told yourself that what others think is crucial and all-important to you, unless you regaled yourself with misbeliefs to the effect that the judgments of other people, particularly if any of them are negative, are much more important than God's approval, unless you have convinced yourself that it is absolutely horrible and tragic if someone doesn't approve of something you do, about all you experienced was some unpleasant feelings.

What if the critic really counts, really has stature? What if the criticisms are right on? Then, of course, you take them and shape your behavior accordingly. That is, you learn from them. No way are such criticisms evil or bad for you. In fact, one reason to go ahead and do the thing you're putting off is so that you can make possible informed criticism by someone who knows what they're talking about.

Procrastination misbelief #11: *I don't feel like doing that now. I shouldn't do such things when I don't feel like it.*

No truly productive person can wait until he "feels like it" to tackle important work. Professional writers produce material on a regular basis, usually working each day, whether they "feel like it" or not. Johann Sebastian Bach, for example, produced his magnificent cantatas at the rate of one each Sunday for five years when he was *Kappelmeister* for St. Thomaskirche, Leipzig. These works had to be completed and rehearsed by musicians and choir for production at the Sunday services. Bach couldn't possibly have worked at his composing only when he felt like it! Yet he produced some of the world's greatest music. It is simply not true that quality work can be produced only when people feel like producing it. The truth is, God has called us to our work, whatever it may be, and has placed us where we are, giving us an opportunity to serve Him and His world by doing what we are called to do. The basis for our activities must be, "Lord, what will *you* have me to do now?" Not, "Hmmm. What do I *feel like* doing now?"

Procrastination misbelief #12: *It's easier not to do it.*

Not so. It's often harder in the long run. Letting it go may be easier *now*, but may cost money (for example in income tax penalties), may create much greater difficulties, may demand more effort, and may cause more total pain in the long run.

There are other reasons we use for putting things off. Your personal procrastination misbeliefs may appear 100 percent reasonable to you at first glance. Sometimes I have to concentrate hard on my own thinking to discover the untruths behind my inaction. I persist because I know these notions are the enemy, or rather they are products of the Enemy's propaganda mills.

If you want to make headway against your own passivity, you will have to recognize that "ideas have consequences." Ideas like these rob you of self-control. Indoctrinated with these lies, you never get around to doing things God has called you to do, even projects you'd really like to carry out. You feel your life is out of control and you are dogged by guilt for not completing the tasks God has set before you.

WHAT TO DO ABOUT PUTTING IT OFF

Here is a step-by-step program for dealing with your own procrastination. We will assume that you are putting off something which has significant consequences for you. You want to overcome your inertia and move on with the fulfillment of your heavenly Father's plan for your life. So what do you do?

Step 1. Start a self-control journal similar to the example in Chapter 3. On the first few pages, list all the things you can think of that you ought to do but don't get around to because they are, for some reason, uninviting to you. You may keep adding to the list as you become aware of postponing something. Include activities you habitually put off, such as returning telephone calls, writing thank-you notes, or changing furnace filters.

Step 2. Read the list over in prayer before the Lord and ask for direction as to what to work on first. Don't try to change everything at once. Refer back to your list during your daily prayer time as a reminder of the project you are working on, as well as a reminder to ask for God's power to overcome and develop control.

Step 3. Use your self-control journal to keep a record of your postponing and what you do about it. Deal with only one project at a time, rather than trying to handle everything at once. Make an entry in your journal *every time* you think about how you really should get started with something you've been putting off. Look again at the sample journal page in Chapter 3 and use it as a model.

To begin each episode, record your "ought thought" as precisely as possible. For example, you may think the words: *You ought to turn off the TV and get the roses covered—winter storms and freezing temps are just around the corner.* Record the words just as you think them.

Then, since you are a skilled procrastinator, you will think a "put-it-off thought," along with one or more misbeliefs to furnish you with the excuses you need to let the roses go. Example: *You don't feel like covering the roses now, and it's not going to freeze tonight, anyhow. Besides, you've been pushing yourself lately and you're tired. You don't have the energy to get out and work in the yard. You need a rest.* Record these thoughts under the heading, *Misbeliefs.*

Third, debate and challenge the misbeliefs you've recorded. Record the debate. Example: *It's a mistake to wait to do everything until I feel like it. Besides, my feelings change often. Many times I haven't felt like working in the yard, and then after getting started I found myself feeling a lot of enjoyment. Whether I enjoy it or not, I don't really want to take a chance on losing those roses and it really could freeze before I get another chance to cover them.*

Fourth, record the truth. Example: *I can and will cover the roses even if I don't "feel like it" right now. I'll feel good about it after I'm done.*

Fifth, act accordingly. Record your action. Example: *Covered roses. Took about twenty minutes.*

PRACTICE

Continue this process, practicing self-control in place of procrastination every day. Check off your list tasks you have successfully completed, such as covering the roses. Also check off habits you have successfully overcome, such as returning phone calls. Continue to add items to your list as they occur to you.

As you do this simple program, you should find yourself much improved in the ability to exercise self-control over previously uncontrolled procrastination. Your written records will very rapidly begin to show fewer and fewer episodes of putting things off, and your master list will become shorter and shorter.

These records are important, not only because they facilitate actually doing something effective about postponing duties, but because they give you feedback and evidence that you are succeeding. This feedback will function as a reward and will encourage and motivate you to continue until you have attained the self-control goal God has set before you.

FIVE

How to Control Your Temper

Have you ever been advised by a well-meaning counselor: *When you are angry, let it out—with feeling*? These counselors think of angry feelings as if they were steam in a boiler, which can build up to dangerous pressure levels. Therefore, blasting other people with vigor is good for you, according to this theory.

Compare the teaching of God's Word on the same subject:

> A fool gives full vent to his anger, but a wise man quietly holds it back. (Prov. 29:11, RSV)

Giving full vent to anger is what we usually mean when we speak of *losing your temper*, or *having a temper tantrum*.

The findings of contemporary psychology, based on numerous, carefully conducted experiments,[1] support the teaching of the Book of Proverbs. True, you may feel some temporary relief from blasting off. But these studies strongly suggest that when people are encouraged to "let it all hang out," they actually become more angry more often. Recently, psychologists have done fresh work on the problem of temper control.

---

[1] Albert Bandura, *Aggression, a Social Learning Analysis* (Englewood Cliffs, New Jersey: Prentice-Hall, 1973).

I'VE TRIED—IT'S NOT SO EASY!

Most Christians will agree with the teaching of Proverbs. We say, "I should control my anger. I shouldn't have temper tantrums. I shouldn't get so worked up over things. I wish I didn't have painful feelings of resentment poisoning my insides. *But it's not so easy!*"

Maybe you've found, too, that it's not so easy to get your anger under control. In fact, your experience might agree precisely with that of Mr. Polwarth in George MacDonald's great novel, *The Curate's Awakening*,[2] "The more I tried, the less I could subdue the wrath in my soul," laments Polwarth.

Perhaps you have made solemn promises to God, family and friends, to improve your disposition. You've clenched your teeth and summoned the force of your will to control your anger. You have tried forgiving those who have hurt you. So far, nothing has worked and you're discouraged and disillusioned.

Mr. Polwarth goes on to describe his despair after trying to force his ugly negative feelings to obey his will. "I hated [my angry feelings], yet could not free myself from them," he explains.

Then he gleefully recounts the discovery which set him free. Mr. Polwarth found an answer in his New Testament. God himself named Jesus the One who would save His people from their sins (Matt. 1:21). The Holy Spirit showed him this meant that Jesus is the Savior, not merely from the *punishment for* sins, but from the *doing of* them.

"What if," asks Mr. Polwarth, "after all the discoveries are made and all the theories are set up and pulled down . . . the strongest weapon a man can wield is prayer to the One who made him?"

Polwarth's discovery points the way for everyone who has a seemingly unmanageable disposition toward anger.

---

[2]George MacDonald, ed. Michael Phillips, *The Curate's Awakening* (Minneapolis: Bethany House Publishers, 1985), p. 53.

Come to the throne of God. That is the place to begin. Tell God about your anger problem. You may not understand it very well, but tell Him all you can. He will grasp the depths of it far better than any psychologist. Then, tell Him you have come to the end of your own resources and have not been able to whip your emotions and actions into line. Ask Him to put to death in you the workings and deeds of the flesh, and to effect the control you need by the power of His indwelling Holy Spirit. As you pray, remind yourself that Jesus died to give you victory over this evil in your life.

BUT—I'VE ALREADY PRAYED

If you have prayed for miraculous temper control, and nothing obvious has yet happened, consider this: The Spirit of truth may be working in the circumstances of your life to teach you self-management skills. Perhaps you need abilities you can gain only through learning— habits which will enable you to cope with difficult situations yet to come. Prayer is first, but it is not necessarily the end of the story. You will most often need training and practice, too, to acquire self-control over angry feelings and actions.

THE NEXT STEP—LET'S LOOK AT ANGER[3]

After you've asked God to work the spiritual fruit of self-control over this domain of your behavior, the next step is to look carefully at what you are actually dealing with.

---

[3]The work of Dr. Raymond Novaco has greatly increased my understanding of anger. The remainder of Chapter 6 reflects some of his thought. See, for example, Dr. Novaco's article in *Cognitive Behavior Therapy: Research and Application*, published by Plenum Press, New York: 1978, Foreyt, John P. and Rathjen. Diana P., editors.

TAKING ANGER APART

What is anger, anyway? To better understand our work, let's take an episode of anger out of life and analyze it into its component parts.

Psychologists define anger in neutral-sounding terms. For instance:

> Anger is an emotional response to one's beliefs about certain environmental events construed as provocations.

Stop! There is no *direct* relationship between environmental events and the emotional response of anger. In order to get angry at all, you have to consider the environmental event, decide that it's a provocation, and then tell yourself certain things about it. In other words, *events don't make us angry. We make ourselves angry by what we believe and tell ourselves about events.* That understanding is critical for our purposes.

AN EPISODE OF ANGER

Once when I'd addressed a group of people, I closed the talk and asked the audience for questions. A middle-aged man asked, "How can I get my fifteen-year-old granddaughter to read your books? I know they'd help her, but I haven't been able to make her read them."

"How old did you say she is? Fifteen?" Intending a bit of humor about adolescent behavior, I said, frivolously, "Just put the books up on a high shelf and tell her she must not look at them. She'll be sure to want to read them."

The audience chuckled—but the questioner didn't. After the session, he came forward with fury in his eye. "You made fun of me," he accused. "You made them all laugh at me. You didn't help me one bit. My granddaughter is a good girl. She isn't like you said at all. Our family doesn't operate that way. You've made me mad."

I was stunned, tried to apologize, to take it all back and start over, but the gentleman would not be mollified. To this day, I feel bad about it.

I can't, however, buy the man's accusation: "You've made me mad." I believe he made himself mad by some things he did mentally with what I said—just as I believe every episode of anger is a result of what we do with environmental events, rather than a direct result of the events themselves. As we look at the following steps, please remember that these mental activities often occur with lightning speed, much faster than we can describe them, or notice them occurring.

First, my erstwhile friend had to *assess* my reply and determine that it was a *provocation*. I hadn't meant it that way at all. He had to say to himself something like this: "He's making fun of me. He wants to make me feel bad in front of all these people. How cruel and heartless. His words are harmful to me."

Second, the man had to compare my reply with his *expectations*. Doubtless he had expected something entirely different, and told himself how wide of the mark I'd fallen. He believed I should have lived up to his expectations and that I should not have answered him as I did.

Third, he had to *evaluate* my words. Something like, "How outrageous of him to be so thoughtless. It's infuriating." Thus he had to assign a great deal of negative importance to them. If he had thought it all a very small matter, he could not have become angry.

Fourth, he had to *give himself permission* to become angry and then *decide* to get upset. "I have every right to be upset about this." Many people deny that they take this step, and most do not notice themselves doing so.

Fifth, following these four steps, his autonomic nervous system responded, and he felt the familiar, unpleasant tightness in his muscles, pounding of his pulses, hot flush on his face, and clenching of his features, which he had learned to identify as *anger*.

Sixth, he labeled his reactions *anger*, talked to himself about how angry I had made him, and thus increased the intensity of his feelings. Here we have what some psychologists call a *feedback loop*, because the process of self-talk increases feelings that, in turn, stoke the self-talk, which again intensifies the feelings, and so on. The result is a vicious circle or a loop that can go on for a very long time. When it continues for long enough, we begin to call it resentment, chronic anger, or bitterness.

Seventh, he expressed his anger. Some people do this by yelling, breaking things, and/or hitting people. Others, by simply telling the offender how they feel (as the man in our story did). Some people express anger by silence or pouting. And some express anger in disguises so arcane and mysterious others can hardly recognize it, let alone guess what the cause is. *Temper oubursts, rage, bad disposition, bad moods, getting even,* and *sarcasm* are examples.

IT HAPPENS SO FAST, YOU THINK YOU CAN'T HELP IT

Most of this occurs in much less time than it takes to read about it. You open the door, discover the mess in the kids' room, and in the twinkling of an eye, you're yelling in rage. You don't even notice the seven steps you took to get yourself upset.

Because anger occurs so rapidly, almost before they know it, people commonly think they cannot control their temper outbursts, bad moods, or bitter, resentful behavior. Often they deny that they talk themselves into anger because they don't notice the lightning-quick inner monologue which brings it on.

So they "explain" their uncongenial ways with one of the standard excuses. Most of us have heard them all, perhaps even used some of them. "I'm Irish so I have a temper!" Some people blame their premenstrual syndrome; others blame the weather. "I have a chemical imbalance" or "I'm hypoglycemic" seems to make many people feel better about their ugly explosions. And, of course, more than anything else, the angry person holds his environment responsible: "It's this weather. It drives me up a wall!" "If you had my kids you'd be cross too!"

Nor do I want to give the impression that the conditions mentioned have nothing to do with temper outbursts, crabbiness, and irritability. Biological and chemical conditions *do* increase the temptation to "let others have it." Stress from any source *does* make it more difficult to control your anger. The error is to believe that these conditions *make* you explode. You do that yourself.

WHAT YOU CAN DO ABOUT ANGER

Take responsibility. Instead of blaming other people and existing conditions, you must learn to take responsibility for your own anger and temper outbursts. That is the first step toward self-control. In prayer, tell the Lord you no longer want to shift blame or try to justify your anger. Instead, you want to receive His righteousness, given freely by virtue of the atoning death of Jesus. Tell Him you intend to accept responsibility for your angry feelings, temper tantrums, and moodiness. Ask for the strengthening power of the Holy Spirit to enable you to exercise self-control in this area.

Nothing is more satisfying and health-giving than learning to control your explosions of wrath and/or your cranky moods.

Loren lost several management jobs on account of his

bad temper. Six months after he was threatened with another termination, he learned how to control his outbursts and went on to a promotion.

Janelle had long disliked herself because of her irascible moods. When she became aware that her children visited friends merely to avoid being in the house with her, she decided something had to be done. Acquiring new control, she discovered a very attractive new self beneath the cover of chronic anger she had worn for years.

Leon stopped using alcohol, but didn't know how to handle the angry feelings he had previously dampened with vodka. His feelings of shame and guilt over the way he was treating others, now experienced full blast, became a powerful temptation to resort to the bottle for soothing. Instead, he worked on developing self-control—an improvement, not only for himself, but for his family as well. It all began when Leon took responsibility instead of shifting blame to other people and things.

Learn specific techniques for relaxation. So intimate is the relationship between temper and tension, tight muscles and crotchety attitudes, it's imperative for anybody with an anger problem to acquire relaxation skills. You can even look at anger as an emotional alarm, alerting you to stress and tension—insisting that *you need to relax.*

Training in relaxation skills is beyond the scope of this book. Most psychologists and some other counselors are equipped to offer training in muscle relaxation. Excellent tapes are available for this purpose, and they are nearly as effective and much less expensive than professional time.[4]

---

[4]One caution: Some professionals have incorporated non-Christian religious and occult elements into their training programs. Transcendental Meditation, spirit communication, and drug states are inappropriate for Christians and contribute nothing to the effectiveness of relaxation training. Try to obtain services and/or training materials from a Christian therapist if at all possible. If not, exercise caution and ask questions. One very simple method of relaxation can be learned from the book, *The Relaxation Response,* by Herbert W. Benson (New York, New York: William Morrow and Co., 1975).

Increasing evidence suggests that aerobic exercise destroys tension and combats stress. Aerobic exercise involves sustained repetitive movement, not brief bursts of strenuous activity. Thus, anti-tension benefits are greatest from such pursuits as walking (for 30-60 minutes a day), running, bicycling, cross-country (not downhill) skiing, and aerobic dancing. (Most of these should be done for a minimum of twenty minutes three times a week.) Booklets giving detailed instructions on aerobic exercise are available free or at minimal expense from the American Heart Association.[5] It is customary to advise people who are not accustomed to exercise, not in good health, or over forty to consult a physician before beginning any exercise program. Start slowly, do not push yourself beyond conservative limits, and cool down after hard exercise by walking for five to ten minutes.

Any reader who has a problem with tension-related emotions—anger, frustration, temper, nervousness, anxiety—may benefit from eliminating or greatly reducing caffein intake. If you decide to kick this drug, expect to feel somewhat sluggish or headache-ridden for a few days. These withdrawal symptoms are generally unpleasant but harmless. Be sure to note that coffee is not the only source of caffein in most homes. Many soft drinks and some headache remedies contain significant amounts of it.

Start an anger journal. The increased self-monitoring necessitated by careful journal-keeping is a vital and important step toward control of anger. In and of itself, keeping a record of an unwanted behavior tends to cause you to reduce the frequency and intensity of the behavior, *even if you don't do any other part of the program.* Furthermore, if you don't record your angry episodes when they occur,

---

[5]Lenore R. Zehman, M.D., *Exercise Your Way to Fitness and Heart Health.*

you will tend to underestimate and/or forget them. That's just human nature.

HOW TO KEEP AN ANGER JOURNAL

Record every episode of anger, no matter how slight its intensity. Begin with date, day, and time.

At first, you should concentrate on learning to notice the *provocations*. That's what we will call the environmental event which precipitates your anger, the occurrence you get upset about. Just describe in neutral, nonjudgmental terms what the other person did or said to give you occasion for anger. Next, write what you did with your anger, whether you told someone off, kicked the dog, stuffed your anger, pouted, or whatever. Finally, record a number between 1 and 10 that represents how intense your anger was on this occasion. (one = barely perceptible irritation; ten = the most intense fury you can imagine.)

Here is a sample episode from a hypothetical anger journal:

May 8

2:40 p.m.

Provocation: Travis wouldn't let me borrow his car. Made some excuse. I've always loaned my things to him.

Behavior: I stuffed it.

Intensity level of anger: 6

Keep your record faithfully for a week. At the end of that time, total up the number of episodes you've logged. That number will serve as a baseline. You will use it later to determine whether you are successfully changing your angry behavior and feelings as we go along.

Use your journal to get a clearer understanding of your problem. Now you can answer for yourself questions like: At whom do I most often become angry? At what events do I become angry? What is the average intensity of my angry feelings?[6] In what situations do I get angry? You must learn these things about yourself so you can learn to prepare in advance for likely precipitants and get yourself ready to react without anger.

EXPANDING YOUR JOURNAL ENTRIES

Use your anger notebook to continue your journal. Keep on making an entry each time you feel any anger. But now begin adding to each entry a note on *how you assessed the provocation event, what your expectations were,* and *how you evaluated the irritant.* Here is the same anger journal page we displayed before, only this time the *assessment, expectations,* and *evaluation* are added. You will probably recognize that these items are elements of self-talk, words and sentences in your internal monologue. It is these words and sentences and others like them which we reiterate to make ourselves angry.

May 8

2:40 p.m.

Provocation: Travis wouldn't let me borrow his car. Made some excuse. I've always loaned my things to him.

Assessment: I took it personally, telling myself Travis is putting me down and insulting me by not trusting me with his car.

Expectations: I had expected Travis to lend me his car because I had loaned my things to him. *He ought to,* I thought.

Evaluation: I told myself it was an important issue, a big deal.

Behavior: I stuffed it.

Intensity level of anger: 6

---

[6]Compute the average by adding up the numbers you assigned to your episodes and divide that sum by the total number of episodes you logged. Later you can compare this first average with the average intensity of your feelings after you have worked on your anger for a few weeks. In this way, you can document your growth in self-control.

Keep your journal like this for one week. At the end of that time, count your anger episodes and determine the average intensity level. Has your anger changed any? Are the episodes more or less frequent? Is the average intensity greater or less? It is entirely possible that you will by now have diminished the intensity and lessened the frequency of your angry episodes. Even if you don't see much change yet, keep working.

The most powerful steps you can take are yet to come.

JOURNALING THE TRUTH

The next step is to record the truth in your journal. It is the truth, according to Jesus, that really sets people free, and the truth about anger is no exception.

Notice particularly your assessments, your expectations, and your evaluations. Careful attention to them will usually reveal that you have distorted the truth in one or more of these items. For example, look again at the sample journal page above. What about the *assessment*? Was it necessary to conclude that Travis's refusal was a *personal* affront or attack? Try an alternative assessment. This, for instance: "It probably isn't true that Travis doesn't trust me particularly. He just has a rule against lending his car out to anyone, and he always sticks to his rules, no matter what. He's never lent his car to anyone, and he doesn't have to. It's his to do with as he likes. I don't need to take this personally."

Can we do anything with *expectations*? Remember, we are most often made angry by our expectations when they are at variance with what actually happens. Here is a possible truthful alternative to the expectations in our example: "Just because I've loaned things freely doesn't mean someone else must act the same way. My behavior isn't the law of God for others. People don't have to do everything the way I do. My lending isn't any basis for concluding that Travis 'ought to' lend his things to me."

Finally, *evaluations* are often distorted in the direction of making events more significant, important, and devastating than they actually are. Generally, we can truthfully modify our anger-arousing evaluations. Like this: "I've overevaluated Travis's refusal. It's really no big deal. I would rather have borrowed the car, but I don't have to have my way all the time. And it isn't an outrage that Travis didn't give me my way."

Once more, let's look at a sample journal page, this time it's complete with the truth.

May 8

2:40 p.m.

Provocation: Travis wouldn't let me borrow his car. Made some excuse. I've always loaned my things to him.

Assessment: I took it personally, telling myself Travis is putting me down and insulting me by not trusting me with his car.

Alternative: Travis never lends his car to anyone. It's not just me. I don't have to take it personally. He always sticks to his rules. And it is his car.

Expectations: I had expected Travis to lend me his car because I had loaned my things to him. *He ought to,* I thought.

Alternative: Others don't have to act the way I do. My behavior doesn't create a law for others.

Evaluation: I told myself it was an important issue, a big deal.

Alternative: I've overevaluated. It's no big deal. No outrage.

Behavior: I stuffed it.

Intensity level of anger: 6

Keep your journal like this for one week. Practice substituting truthful alternatives for the old, anger-arousing assessments, expectations and evaluations. At the end of that time, again count the number of episodes and compute average intensity. You will begin to find that both frequency and intensity of anger have been reduced through telling yourself the truth. Continue keeping your anger journal until the habits of analyzing your anger and telling yourself the truth become automatic.

STUFFING IT

Now we take a look at the issue of overt behavior, that is, what you *do* about it when you've upset yourself over something.

What *should* you do when you feel angry at another person? Stuff it? Some Christians have argued that one ought always to refuse anger any channel of outward expression. These believers point to the thoughts of the Apostle James concerning anger. James notes that human anger does not work the righteousness of God. Expressing anger can be a spiritually risky business, that is true.

Yet, many have noted that stuffing anger also leads to bad results. Anger-stuffers become moody, stubborn, silent and difficult. They may deliberately come late for appointments, stubbornly sabotage your best efforts to get along with them, or criticize incessantly. And, worse, they may barely know they are angry. The words of the Apostle Paul in Ephesians teach that one needs to express anger and get the issue resolved immediately. Paul advises, "Be angry, but do not sin. Do not let the sun go down on your anger" (Eph. 4:26).

So what should you do? Suppress it or express it? Shut up or blow up? I've worked on this question for many years, and I must tell you that there are times when I'm not sure. On some occasions, I don't know for certain whether to deal with the provocation in the environment or only with myself. Of course, both Paul and James are teaching God's truth. But the problem is when to be angry and take it up with the other person, and when to quietly change your own self-talk so as not to allow yourself to get angry.

As is so often the case when people disagree, both sides have a point. There are situations when it is best not to express anger and there are other situations in which it is downright wrong to fail to express it truthfully, openly, directly, with a request that the other person change some behavior.[7] The Spirit of Truth will help you decide in each case whether the situation calls for truthful expression of anger to another, or changing your own misbelieving self-talk. Most often, I have come to believe, it is imperative to work on *yourself* when you are angry. Especially if you find yourself losing your cool very frequently.

To simply "stuff it" when you're angry is never an adequate, God-pleasing, or healthy tactic. On those occasions when you believe it is *not* God's will for you to express your anger directly to the other person, you must work very hard to deal with your own emotions so that those emotions will not damage your body or your relationships with others and with God. And even when you believe God wants you to express your anger to someone, you need to have your anger under control so it doesn't control you. An intemperate outburst is never desirable and can have untold negative consequences.

LEARNING TO COPE

How do some people manage to handle life's provocations without getting upset? Have you asked yourself that question repeatedly without finding an answer? Perhaps you've heard sermons or read books advising you to control your anger without much in the way of concrete instructions on how to do it. Maybe you've already picked up on the secret: Learn to tell yourself the truth in place of the anger-breeding misbeliefs you discovered as you kept your journal. You might even have learned what the

---

[7]For a fuller treatment, see William Backus, Ph.D., *Telling Each Other the Truth* (Minneapolis: Bethany House Publishers, 1985).

truth actually *is* in irritating situations hitherto inflamed by misbeliefs.

So let's say you come to the point where you have reduced the frequency and intensity of your anger eruptions through prayerful journal-keeping and forcing yourself to look at the truth, but there are still occasions when you lose your temper or become aggravated before you know what hit you. Now, you want to know how to prepare beforehand so you can keep from getting upset in provocative situations.

STEP ONE: BRIEF YOURSELF IN ADVANCE

As you learn to know yourself more intimately through the work of journaling, you will come to foresee provoking situations before they occur: the man at work who always manages to "get your goat"; the business associate with whom you rarely see eye-to-eye; the woman at church who always has a critical remark. Often we can predict ahead of time that a situation might become irritating. That means we can, if we know how, brief ourselves in advance so that we're all ready to meet it without boiling over.

You can memorize the words I gave to one client and use them for a while. Later, you can modify them to more closely fit your needs and the peculiarities of your difficult interpersonal situations. Here they are:

> This meeting (date, discussion, class session, etc.) could be pretty difficult. But I'm going prepared this time and I've learned to manage such things a lot better than I used to. God's Holy Spirit, the Spirit of Truth, lives within. With His help, I can work out the truth I'm going to tell myself so I can manage this. Calm down! Whatever I do I mustn't take things personally, but stick to the points in question. This doesn't have to turn into a quarrel. I've acquired the skills to do this right. God will help me to handle it.

My client reported that she felt better and less tense

in provocative situations, just because she had armed herself in advance with this internal speech.

STEP TWO: WHEN THE IRRITANT HAPPENS

You are now in the worrisome situation and, sure enough, the person who has gotten you upset many times before actually does his thing again. But you are prepared. Here is what you can tell yourself when the irritant actually occurs:

> I can control myself here. I've learned how to do it. Dwelling within me is God's own Spirit, the Giver of self-control. I can stay calm and cool and as long as I do that, I'm in control of myself and the situation. I don't have to convince anybody of anything. I don't have to make others believe I'm worthwhile. No point in escalating this, no sense getting angry. That isn't going to work the righteousness of God. I'm going to think of the steps I need to take to handle this, look for what's good in the situation, and refuse to jump to conclusions.

Again, you can adapt these words to fit your situations better. After many repetitions, the thoughts will occur automatically.

STEP THREE: HOW TO HANDLE ANGRY FEELINGS

One important aim in a provocative situation is to prevent a feedback loop from getting started. A feedback loop, you may recall, is activated when a person senses the first bodily components of anger in himself, talks himself into more anger, feels the increased intensity, increases his angry self-talk, and so on. We "work ourselves up" to fury if we keep going. You can learn some new self-talk, designed to prevent a feedback loop. Say to yourself, the moment you notice any of the physical reactions typical of the emotion of anger:

> I can feel my heartbeat speeding up. Calm down, re-

lax, take it easy. Take a deep breath. I want to look at this as a problem to be solved, not as an outrage to be reacted to. The anger I'm feeling means it's time to look for solutions and to work things out. He/she may be trying to get me angry, but I want to respond in the righteousness of God, and I'm going to look for a resolution we'll both feel good about later.

Talk to yourself this way the moment you first feel your breathing quicken, muscles tense, or heart beat faster in anger. Soon you'll discover that you can make yourself relaxed and calm. In this state, you will feel level-headed and in better control of yourself because you are no longer being carried away by feelings.

STEP FOUR: REVIEWING HOW WELL YOU DID

The provocative situation is over. Too often, before working on control, you may find yourself chewing over angry, bitter self-talk for hours, and even days. Some of us just can't forget the irritation. This gnawing resentment can brew, especially if you and the other person weren't able to work things out. Eventually you can learn to tell yourself truths like the following as you mull over provoking events later:

You don't have to dwell on him and on what he did. Especially, you don't have to keep telling yourself how terrible it all is. It's very likely not such a big deal, and will all be forgotten in time. Anyway, his behavior is his problem so you can quit taking it personally. Quit rehearsing the irritant because doing so only upsets you. Take ten minutes to relax all your muscles. Then forget about it. Get your mind on your work or something else. Let the Holy Spirit work thoughts in you that will lead to the righteousness of God instead of the anger of man.

WHEN YOU HAVE A SUCCESS

God is the source of the spiritual fruit of self-control—but you are the one who must exercise the self-control you've been given. It is not Christian modesty, but error and falsehood, to pretend that you had nothing to do with it when you manage yourself well. Be sure to reward yourself when you succeed in dealing with an irritating situation effectively and with a good handle on your anger. Tell yourself something like this after it's all over and you can see that you carried out your anger-control program:

> I can hear the Lord saying, "Well done!" And I did do a pretty good job. Jerry's remark could have set my self-talk going until I really upset myself. But instead of grinding my innards to powder, I made myself recognize the truth: It was no big deal—not worth all the tension. My envy can turn my head around, but I'm getting better. I got through it without getting mad. Praise God!

BUT THIS IS TOO HARD!

One of the most prevalent misbeliefs among people with deficits in self-control is the conviction that anything worthwhile should be easy, as we noted earlier. "Things shouldn't be so hard." "A counselor should be able to get rid of my bad temper without a whole lot of effort on my part." These are misbeliefs, and by labelling them so, I aim to emphasize how utterly false they are. Most people who have managed to grow and improve the quality of their behavior have had to exert tremendous effort. Most worthwhile accomplishments, whether they be changing conditions or changing oneself, have involved enormous expenditures of time and effort. If it's worth doing, it's worth doing with effort. And nearly anything worthwhile requires that effort.

I realize many Christians think prayer provides a shortcut, an effortless method of getting things done. And sometimes prayer does accomplish wonders without our effort. However, prayer is not a shortcut for everything, not a device for getting through life without any personal involvement, commitment, or strain.

The program of prayerful journal-keeping and self-monitoring described in this chapter does require effort. But it will pay rich dividends and will afford the sense of wholeness to the person who has himself well in hand. Learning to tell yourself the truth and thus to handle previously upsetting situations with Christian aplomb is a sure sign of maturing—and a source of great freedom and happiness. Why not get started on that temper right now?

SIX

Does Your Sex Drive Manage You?

I can still hear the pleading note in Mal's voice as he recounted for me his last conversation with his girlfriend, Ellen. They had hashed over her refusal to have sex with him for what seemed like the ninety-ninth time. "I'm a normal guy, for cryin' out loud! What am I suppose to do for sex?" he had demanded of her. How could she really love him and still resist him as consistently as she did? Could she be frigid?

As I listened to Mal, I thought of other men and women who have come to me seeking help with problems related to out-of-control sexuality.

There was Mark and Anita, struggling to keep themselves "pure" until their wedding night; Warren, high up in a major political party, anxious that he would not be able to perform like a sexual machine when the women he dated demanded sex; Gary, a young man who had become impotent because he feared he would not be the perfect lover; Karen, who defiantly insisted, "There's nothing wrong with having sex with someone you love"—but despised herself.

The idea of self-control was a problem for each of these single folks, trying to survive in today's permissive culture.

Nor is it any less a stumbling block for some married

people. I think of Ted, whose thoughtless, self-gratifying appetites caused him nearly to rape his wife every night, causing her to hate him *and* sex; and Liz, who gave free reign to her sexual fantasies—no matter how deviant—until they drove her into affairs with fellow employees, neighbors and even men at church. At last her embittered husband divorced her.

Clinicians encounter a veritable weed-garden of failed self-control among married people. Adulterous affairs are most common. Demands for partner participation in forms of sex that offend are common, too. Compulsive masturbation by one or the other partner may lead to avoidance of intercourse and disruption of the marital relationship. Sometimes one partner may act out in deviant sexual patterns (homosexuality, cross-dressing, exhibitionism, voyeurism, child molesting, incest), demanding in the name of love that the spouse accept the perverse behavior as harmless fun, thus becoming an enabler. Each time I hear one of these sad stories, I am impressed again with the realization that sexual dyscontrol can make wreckage of precious human lives.

As this book is written, an outbreak of a sexually transmitted killer disease, Acquired Immune Deficiency Syndrome (AIDS), has begun to destroy human lives in every part of the world. No cure exists, and the disease, invariably fatal, has begun to spread like wildfire through even the heterosexual population. No preventive measures are totally effective. The only way to prevent sexual transmission of the AIDS virus is to practice the chastity of sexual life commanded by God thousands of years ago.

The sexual prohibitions of God's Word weren't given to spoil man's fun, but to preserve health and sexual vitality. All these people had listened, consciously or unconsciously, both to their own sinful impulses and urges, and to the propaganda of anti-Christian thought-shapers who reiterate *ad nauseam* how sexual urges need not be controlled and how it is unhealthy to suppress them. Today's permissive philosophies are blind to the human sadness they wreak.

Let's look at a case in point.

BRANDON

Brandon came to me after the state board of dentistry ordered him to seek psychological treatment. Brandon, though not a believer himself, appeared especially curious about my commitment to Jesus Christ. But I am getting ahead of my story.

"You probably know why I'm here," he began. He covered his embarrassment by lolling back in the recliner, trying to appear relaxed, at ease. His words were a feeler.

Yes, I knew what sort of trouble he was in. The local newspapers had reported, as headline news, the fact that Brandon had been barred from practicing dentistry because he had been "sexually victimizing" many of his female patients. Now his marriage, his profession and his potential financial ruin hung upon the result of his finding treatment that would help him control his behavior. Nonetheless, I asked him to give me his story himself.

With far more poise than I could have exhibited in his shoes, Brandon said he'd realized that one day his sexual activities with patients would end in disaster. So he'd made resolutions and vows to himself, tried everything he knew to stop.

"But Bill," he pleaded, "some of them wouldn't quit. They made passes at me nobody could resist. The same woman who reported me to the board of dentistry had come right out and invited me to go to bed with her. What was I supposed to do?" he demanded, sitting upright in the chair. "I'm only human."

If Brandon felt any shame or guilt, he masked it under a mixture of social aplomb and offense at the very idea that a professional board could wreak such havoc in a man's life. I suspected that his tactic of blaming others kept his own ego from experiencing any real conviction of wrongdoing. I figured that at this point his concern was the trouble he was in rather than conscience pangs. Not a good sign.

Therefore, I didn't think psychology alone would be able to give him what he needed. It was my opinion that Brandon would find little permanent help unless he went through repentance to the cross of Jesus Christ. A new birth of faith in Christ as Savior and Lord was the only deep cure I knew of for his weakened conscience and uncontrolled impulses.

MISBELIEFS DESTROY SEXUAL SELF-CONTROL

In the course of our counseling, I was curious to know why Brandon was seemingly unable to control his destructive sexual behavior. We delved into his history and explored his reflections about his own actions. It soon became apparent that his misbehavior was the result of long-held misbeliefs about sex, about himself, and about the meaning and value of other people.

We'd been exploring his notions about right and wrong sexuality one day when he exploded. "Bill, I can't make any sense out of your notion that my values are wrong. They're values, man! Nobody can prove values right or wrong!"

I plied him. "Are you saying it seems incredible to you that some things can be true in such an absolute sense that things contrary to them are downright false?"

"To me," he shot back, "when you say a behavior is right or wrong, you're only describing how you personally feel about it. You're referring to your own subjective state of approval or disapproval—like saying you like vanilla and dislike chocolate."

Instead of arguing with him, I sought the Lord prayerfully. Brandon obviously did not believe in absolutes, yet he had made it a point to say he had come to me because

I am a Christian psychotherapist. Now the Holy Spirit seemed to confirm my guess that Brandon had sought me because he was really hungry for the Bread of Life.

"Brandon," I challenged him, "we're coming from different places. There isn't any point in our arguing about values. Instead, why don't you tell me why you decided to consult me instead of someone whose values would be more like yours?"

Brandon readily admitted that he knew he "needed something more" in his life. He was ready to find God, if for no reason more noble than his deep, underlying despair, which was beginning to show in his eyes.

For the next couple of sessions, we discussed Jesus Christ, God's answer to human bondage. I showed him how Jesus came to bring about freedom, not only from the penalty for sin, but from the power of sin as well. Taking the first steps of faith, he laid his sins before God, and received forgiveness and a life-changing new birth by accepting Jesus Christ as Savior and Lord.

Since he now knew the Absolute himself, Brandon slowly began to accept absolute truths—God's truths—about right and wrong behavior. Now we could explore some of the misbeliefs that had destroyed his sexual self-control.

Some will insist that the new birth of faith in Christ should suffice to destroy Brandon's sinful habits and set his feet on the path of truth in every area of his life. But those with more experience in Christian living and in counseling others will recognize that becoming a Christian doesn't automatically purge all the falsehood out of a person's belief system, any more than it renders a person instantly perfect. The life after new birth is a process of growth in grasping and living the truth.

Eventually, his license restored, Brandon returned to his practice. He reported that the nature of his relationship with patients had changed considerably, and that though he felt some of the old temptations, he also felt able to stand against them. I haven't seen Brandon for some time, but I know he's still practicing dentistry, and I haven't seen his name in the paper. So far, so good.

I have briefly recounted Brandon's experience to illustrate dramatically how important it is to begin this kind of therapy with a deep commitment to Jesus Christ and His will. In order to examine the unravelling of sexual misbeliefs, let's look at another case.

JOY

I'll never forget the puzzlement and frustration I saw in Joy during our first interview. She was twenty-seven, auburn-haired, easy on the eyes and unmarried. She yearned for a husband and children with all her heart—and she realized her promiscuity was thwarting the attainment of her goals.

"I don't want to go to bed with every guy I date," Joy complained, "but no matter how hard I try, I can't seem to help it. What's wrong with me? Am I 'oversexed' or something? Why do I feel so helpless with men?"

"I can't say no," Joy continued tearfully as I encouraged her to talk freely about her problem. "I tell myself over and over again that I don't want to give in this time. But if the guy comes on strong, I cooperate—even if I don't like him very much. I just don't have any willpower. The next morning, I look in the mirror and tell myself I'm a slut.

"Oh, sometimes I do say 'No' pretty softly, so I'm not very convincing. Men seem to take it as an incentive to push harder, and, instead of pulling back, they literally force me into bed. When I read a magazine article on *date rape,* the forcing of sex on an unwilling friend during a date, I realized I'm a frequent victim!

"It's so bad I feel like not dating anybody. I don't know what to do. I just can't handle men, I guess."

"When a man is pushing you to have sex with him and

you're trying to say no without much success, what's going on in your mind at that time?" I pursued.

She thought about it for a few seconds and shrugged. "I don't think about anything in particular."

Many clients say they don't have any special thoughts during the difficult moments when they are torn by conflict between their desire to control themselves and the impulse to let go and repeat some bit of self-defeating behavior. Nevertheless, when they make an effort to pay attention to their thoughts in the throes of the struggle, they discover mental contents they hadn't noticed before. Joy agreed to pay close attention to her own internal monologue the next time she found herself fighting the battle over sexual control.

As the opening line of our next session, Joy said miserably, "It happened again. I gave in. I was hoping this time I could say no and mean it, you know, with my treatment and all. No such luck."

"Joy, God can even turn this into something valuable," I asserted. "Tell me, did you focus your attention on your internal monologue?"

"Yes," she said slowly. Then she took a notebook from her handbag. "I remembered to do what you told me to. I even wrote it down. Want to hear it?"

I nodded, and she began to read.

> He's expecting me to go to bed with him. I know I shouldn't. But how can I tell him? It's too late for him to stop now, isn't it? I've already let him kiss me and touch me all over and he's turned on. If I refuse him now he's going to be furious.

Suddenly, she stopped reading. Looking at me nervously, she hurried to explain. "I can't stand it when guys get mad at me. I don't know why—it ties me in knots. And I'm always afraid of upsetting them—you know, when they're so frustrated—so I decide it's easier to give in one more time and get it over with."

"You tell yourself you can't stand a man's anger?" I offered.

"Right. I don't know why I get so panicky when a man—any man—is displeased with me. I used to be terrified of my father. He'd fly into a rage, break furniture, and stop talking to everybody in the family. We were all miserable for days. So we learned to walk on eggshells when Dad was home. We had to avoid upsetting him at all costs."

I said it sounded to me as though she had no choice in those days but to suffer all that tyrannical abuse along with the rest of the family. "Do you think it's the same now? Don't you have any more choices or freedom than you had at age eight?"

"Well—I suppose—in a way. But I still feel panicky when I think anybody, especially a guy, is going to get upset with me."

I now tried to show Joy that she was needlessly fearful of male anger because she believed and told herself that such anger, like her father's when she was a little girl, would be terrible and harmful to her. At first, Joy had difficulty accepting my assertion that her panic was due to false beliefs. It seemed evident to her that, in some way, an angry male is surely dangerous.

Yet, after we'd worked on this for awhile, the truth began to dawn on her. There wasn't much to fear. Even if a man got upset with her there was little likelihood that he could do her any harm. At last she grasped, at least intellectually, that getting a man upset was hardly the crime of the century.

"I guess if a man gets angry with me now I can stay away from him, can't I?" she concluded. "It wouldn't be the same as it was when I was eight years old, not really. You know, I've tried so hard to please, I've hardly ever let anyone get angry with me. So I really have never had a chance to find out exactly what would happen. I've done whatever men ask to keep them from getting upset. I've just assumed it's the same as it was when I was a child having to please my father."

"But now you can see that your belief is untrue, can't you?" I encouraged her. "You aren't a child and you don't have to please your father or anyone else except the Lord."

She began to get into the spirit of the thing: "So, if I decide to be pure and a man objects, it's too bad. But I don't have to tell myself I can't stand it if he gets mad at me. You know, all these years, I've been assuming I had to keep placating men the way all of our family placated my dad. But I don't! I have a choice. It probably wouldn't be any big deal at all, even if I made a man angry by refusing to have sex with him."

"What would probably happen if you said a firm no and the man reacted angrily?" I asked her.

"Well, I guess he'd probably clam up. Treat me coldly. Maybe just say a curt good night and leave. I might never hear from him. Then again—well, who knows? Maybe he'd stay interested and call me after he cooled off." Joy had never given serious thought to the question of what the actual consequences of refusing sex might be. She was surprised at her conclusions.

"What's so terrible about all that?"

"Nothing."

It would take some experience with masculine anger and with the fact that it could do her little harm before she would lose her anxiety completely. But Joy continued to make an effort to argue against her untruthful beliefs. She would challenge them energetically as they filtered into her mind. Then she would take care to replace them by telling herself something like the following every time she found herself in what we referred to as "the situation":

> I know he could become angry, and I can feel myself tensing up like when I was little and Dad blew up. Calm down. I'm not a child and this guy isn't my dad. Even if he yells or insults me, I can handle it. And he probably won't do anything—maybe just act offended, or just go

home. Even if he doesn't call me again, I can survive. I don't desperately need this man's attention. But I do need to respect myself and see myself as pure and holy. I need to please my Lord Jesus. I am filled with the Holy Spirit, and I can handle this situation.

Joy kept her journal, taking care to record her self-talk at times when she felt tempted to become sexually involved. Very rapidly, she began to gain control. As a matter-of-fact, she reported after the session in which we had first dissected, challenged and replaced her misbeliefs about making men angry that she had successfully resisted the sexual advances of a very attractive man in whom she had considerable interest.

In fact, he'd become quite irritated with her, threatened the relationship, and even suggested that she might be a lesbian. He did not fail to call again, however. When he did, she turned him down, realizing that she did not care to become involved with someone so immature.

Yet, I knew that one victory doesn't win a war and that Joy might very well have some slips. Furthermore, as it turned out, Joy's first misbelief was not the only one we discovered. As she kept her journal, she was able to uncover other misbeliefs governing her sexual behavior. Some of them were overtly present in her self-talk and some of them we had to infer, for though they undergirded and supported her conscious self-talk, they were not themselves present in her consciousness.

As time went on, Joy became more skilled at dealing with sexual advances. She did have more than one slip, particularly with exceptionally aggressive and insistent men. We examined these episodes together, using them to shed light on her vulnerabilities. When I last heard from Joy, she had experienced several months during which she had been in control of her sexual behavior and had had no further slips. The improvement she experienced in her own self-evaluation was so rewarding, I expect her to continue to exercise her newfound self-control.

MISBELIEFS IN SEXUAL DYSCONTROL

Brandon, Joy, and others with sexual control difficulties share some misbeliefs in common. As you study the following summary of misbeliefs held by people with sexual control problems, you can use them to discover your own. There is a good chance yours will be on the list, because these false notions are seldom original. Rather, they are planted by the father of lies, who appears to be anything but creative.

For instance:

Sexual Misbelief #1: *I can't control my sex drive.*

In nearly all self-control issues, poorly controlled people tell themselves, "I can't help it!" "I know I should resist eating chocolate decadence, but I can't resist. I'm powerless." "I know I should quit smoking, but I can't." "When I'm alone with an attractive person of the opposite sex for whom I have strong feelings, I'm gone! I can't help myself."

This misbelief actually facilitates the unwanted behavior. When you can convince yourself you are unable to help what you are about to do, you thereby *become* unable to help it. In fact, there isn't any point in struggling with an issue when the outcome is foreordained! If you can't help it, why try? If you can make yourself believe that you are truly an exceptional person and that you have a massive libido, driven by a force far too strong to master, you can allow yourself to go ahead, to take the easy way out.

But is this old-wheeze of a cliché true? The behavior you say you can't help is performed with muscles controlled voluntarily. It's not a twitch. To climb into bed you have to will certain muscles in your limbs to contract so your legs and arms bend. It is physiological fact that you *can* exert control, that, in fact, you must *decide* to perform the actions in question. Sexual behavior doesn't happen by itself.

People who know Jesus Christ have the Holy Spirit dwelling within them and directing their actions. One result of that indwelling Spirit's work ("the fruit of the Spirit") is the ability to control yourself. Brandon had made himself believe he couldn't help seducing his patients. But when he became a Christian, he had no choice but to revise this notion. He concluded that, in the light of the Word of God, it couldn't be true.

If you have Jesus Christ as Savior and Lord, you *do* have the power to control your actions in sexual matters. To confess anything else is to call God a liar. Even if you think your experience teaches you otherwise, you must take the first step out of that pit—and that step is to tell yourself the truth: "I can control my actions in sexually provocative situations. Never again will I tell myself, 'I can't.'"

Sexual Misbelief #2: *Chastity is bad for me.*

You may be telling yourself this one because you read it or heard it somewhere. It is an old notion, coming out of psychological theories devised long ago without the benefit of experimental research. If you believe this old chestnut, you have small incentive to control yourself, because you believe that control is detrimental.

Of course, this lie insinuates that God has really messed things up. Since God commands chastity and self-control in sexual matters, this misbelief actually accuses God of willing something that will harm you. What kind of father do you imagine Him to be—a sadistic tormentor who enjoys watching His family writhe in anguish and self-destruction? What sort of "Good Shepherd" would deliberately direct the sheep to pastures and waters He knew to be poisoned? No way! God gave His best for you, and He consistently does only good. He would never order what is harmful.

Psychology has no facts proving that you do yourself harm if you live without sexual activity. On the contrary, although an enormous amount of research has been done on human sexuality in the last forty years, evidence still fails to confirm the widely held opinion that continence (self-restraint in sexual activity) is bad. Of course, continence is seldom pleasant, comfortable, or easy. And it may be more difficult for some people than for others. But remaining pure will not cause you damage of any kind.

Sexual Misbelief #3: *Having sex with numerous women makes you a real man.*
Sexual Misbelief #4: *Truly liberated women have sex whenever they choose. This is one of the privileges women are entitled to because they are equal with men.*
Sexual Misbelief #5: *You're not normal if you don't have sex regularly. You're weird. Something's wrong with you.*

These three misbeliefs all have the same root: *Sex proves something.* According to this twisted notion, it is an achievement to have sexual intercourse, a greater achievement to have more than one partner, and an even more spectacular feat to sleep with numerous partners. In this way you demonstrate to the world that you are super desirable, loads of fun, free from bothersome hang-ups, as good as anyone else or maybe just a tad better—and very, very normal. If you are a woman, you prove that you are truly liberated and equal with any man. If you are a man, you prove that you are unquestionably masculine—a real hunk.

Using sex to prove something often begins in childhood and adolescence, and is childish behavior at whatever age you do it. When boys start bragging in the locker room and girls recount their loss of virginity in the dorm, it becomes important to be able to talk about one's sexual adventures and amatory prowess to others. Or maybe, for reassurance, to oneself. Now, suddenly, sex becomes, not a gift of God for experiencing oneness, pleasure and parenthood, but a competitive sport to be engaged in for social awards. People telling themselves these misbeliefs are still living by some of the misconceptions of childhood.

It should be obvious from the way I've spelled out these common beliefs that they are far from true. As a matter-of-fact, some research has linked psychological misery and *ab*normality with unrestrained and immoral sexual behavior, while happiness has been linked with purity.[1]

If the perfect model of masculinity is Jesus of Nazareth, the lie is thereby given to such misbeliefs as these. A moment's thought will convince you that having sexual intercourse proves nothing whatever about your human worth, importance, or goodness. Sexual coupling doesn't make you a liberated woman. Christ does. And it doesn't confer masculinity either. It doesn't even prove you have any social or interpersonal desirability.

Sexual Misbelief #6: *Everybody else is enjoying sex immensely, so I'm left out and cheated if I control myself and they don't. It's unfair.*

Sexual Misbelief #7: *Others don't feel cheap and guilty about having sex, and it's unfair that I have such feelings.*

---

[1]O. Hobart Mowrer, *New Evidence Concerning the Nature of Psychopathology*, in Buffalo Studies, Vol. IV, No. 2, August 1968.

Albert Bandura, *Aggression*, a Social Learning Analysis (Englewood Cliffs, New Jersey: Prentice-Hall, 1973).

This is merely a variation on the pervasive misbelief that when anyone else has something I don't have, God has committed a foul. It's monstrously unfair. However, we have no way of knowing for sure what's going on in another person's sex life. We can't tell what others are doing, enjoying, or feeling, so we have to rely on guesses and inferences—unless we're listening to those who brag about their supposed "conquests." When such people tell you what they're doing, you would be wise to notice they're trying to create envy and elicit admiration.

Such motivations may lead to untruthful bragging and boasting. But even if others do have things you lack, or enjoy short-term pleasures you are not free to sample, it makes no sense to envy them because in the long run, their behavior brings negative consequences. It may appear to you as though Mary has all the best. But you could be watching a rerun of the old story of the ant and the grasshopper. Perhaps Mary is living it up these days, while you are restraining your passions and urges with considerable effort and difficulty. But what about the long-term consequences? What is Mary doing to herself? Is she squandering her resources? When the results of her prodigality catch up with her, won't she be far worse off than others who used more restraint? What sense does it make to envy Mary in view of the future? Will she find herself trying to manage as an impoverished single parent? Will she suffer chronic illness from some sexually transmitted disease? Will she face death as a result of contracting AIDS? Will she pass on the infection to countless others—perhaps her own children or her husband? Will she ruin a future marriage by resuming her promiscuous habits?

Particularly when you know God's judgment on uncontrolled sexual behavior—namely, that those who do such things cannot inherit the kingdom of God—it makes no sense to envy the poor soul squandering eternal well-being in exchange for a few orgasms.

As for feelings of guilt, they are appropriate consequences of sinful behavior. If you feel guilt when you sin
and others *say* they don't (remember, others may have
guilt feelings they don't own up to), you are the one who
is better off, even if it's painful. In the same way, a person
whose nervous system is intact feels the pain of injuries
and is therefore much more fortunate than the person who
cannot feel pain due to neurological damage. Pain, though
unpleasant, is a valuable indicator of trouble and a warn-
ing to change something. Guilt feelings in consequence of
truly sinful behavior signal that change is needed to avoid
further spiritual and psychological damage.

Sexual Misbelief #8: *Sex is just a mechan-
ical act having no moral implications per se
unless you spread disease or fail to prevent
conception.*
Sexual Misbelief #9: *Marriage is just a for-
mality, a mere piece of paper; it shouldn't
stand in the way of people enjoying themselves.*

Although these misbeliefs are shattered by the clear
teachings of Scripture, there are people who argue for
them, usually to justify their own sinful sexual behavior.
Today, some church people declare that sexual activity
outside marriage is not wrong—that while the Bible does
teach that sexual intercourse should occur only between
married persons of opposite sexes, this teaching is no
longer appropriate. It *was* valid, long ago, because in
those days contraception was not widely available and
people did not know how to take precautions against venereal diseases. Today, it is argued, we have ready access
to contraceptives and medications for sexually-transmit-
ted diseases, so there is no longer any reason to attach

moral strictures to sexual behavior between consenting persons.

The direct result of this cultural misbelief has been an epidemic of teenage pregnancy, slaughter of the unborn in unprecedented numbers, and an enormous social burden of care for unwed mothers and their children. Recently, new sexually transmitted diseases have surfaced, some of them impossible to cure and one invariably lethal. Unfortunately, those so glued to this cultural misbelief that no array of facts can penetrate their defenses long enough to unstick them continue prescribing more of the same "remedies" with which they compounded the social consequences of immorality in the first place: more "sex education," more "values clarification," more contraceptives, cheaper abortions, and more dollars spent for research into cures for sexually transmitted diseases. What they have not done is come forward to say, "We were wrong." Events, however, have made the point for them. The Word of God is not just another throwaway item in a throwaway culture—like yesterday's newspaper.

The truth is that each sexual act has eternal significance, bonding two individuals together in a union which, whether intended or not, exists with rather serious consequences. Read 1 Cor. 6:15–20 for a more fulsome discussion of this bonding and its implications. For this and other very sound reasons, God is extremely serious about His commandments against impurity, fornication, sexual deviation and adultery.

Sexual Misbelief #10: *Sex is sacred. Everything else should be subordinated to it.*

Every culture needs to enshrine something. The secular culture, in spite of the best efforts of its intellectuals and thought leaders to expunge all religion, cannot help venerating something. So, like the heathen priests of the

Fertile Crescent a thousand years ago, many have chosen to sacralize sex. In spite of enormous consequences in massive social problems, the thought shapers of secular culture continue their dogged insistence that sex is too sacred to criticize. Whatever is done to heal the anguish caused by letting sex reign supreme, it *must not* involve asking anyone to inhibit sexual urges. "Let the entire society perish if it must, but make room for my preferred sexual styles and occasions. Sex is sacred." So goes this misbelief.

The truth is, of course, that sex is not sacred. Only One is holy. Sex is His good creation, but it is not God. If you have made it a god by letting sex rule your life and behavior, you need to discover and tell yourself the truth: sex has its rightful place only when it is subjected to God and His commands.

Sexual Misbelief #11: *Sex is a private matter between you and your (adult) partner and what you do in your bedroom is nobody else's business.*

Nothing could be further from the truth. Even though it is customary to perform sexual intercourse in private, its implications are not private. The belief that sex is a private matter has led to great difficulties for individuals and for society including numerous families without fathers, widespread poverty, and worrisome disease epidemics for which everyone is forced to bear part of the cost. Actually, there is probably no private act with such weighty social repercussions as sexual intercourse. Because, as a Christian, you are responsible for the well-being of the other person, the culture and the world, you really cannot shrug and tell yourself that what you do in the bedroom isn't anyone else's business.

Sexual Misbelief #12: *Having sex is the only way to hang on to a prospective mate; if you don't do it, no one will love you or marry you.*

Sexual Misbelief #13: *The other person wants sex. If you refuse you'll lose him or her, and you can't stand that.*

First, let's acknowledge what fragments of validity these ideas possess. There *are* people who won't pursue a relationship without sex. If you refuse them, they will move on to someone else. They may *say* they are interested in a deep, long-term relationship, even marriage, but they have to check out the quality of a sexual experience with you before they can decide. Or they may *say* they cannot believe you really love them unless you have intercourse with them.

Whatever such people *say* (such talk was known as "a line"), what they *want* is sexual intercourse. There is nothing whatever wrong with that. But they usually want it *now* and without the bother of establishing a marital bond in which sexual intercourse can occur with God's blessing.

So what if one of these people decides you are too stiff and prim, or if they accuse you of being neurotic, abnormal, frigid, or even homosexually perverted? You are better off in the long run if such a person moves on, for to become involved and even married to someone with values so distorted as to clash with God's Word at every step of the way is a recipe for misery.

After many interviews with people who have bought this line and agreed to have sex to hang on to the interest and love of the other person, I have concluded it seldom works. Sex outside of marriage rarely deepens a relationship or increases the interest of another person in you.

You can't make someone want you, or love you, or stick with you by copulating.

Sexual Misbelief #14: *A little sex never hurt anybody. What's the harm when two consenting adults do whatever they feel like doing in private?*

When you find yourself thinking like this, you must remind yourself of the fact that people in such situations are actually being intimate not only with an illicit partner, but with every one of that person's sexual intimates over the past years. This truth has become an issue of life and death since the AIDS plague has radically altered the meaning of casual sex *even for those who care nothing for God's commandments*. A little sex can not only hurt you— it can kill you.

AFTER YOU TELL YOURSELF THE TRUTH, WHAT?

Greta had become discouraged with her lack of progress. She and I had worked together on her sexual self-control problem for seven weeks, and Greta had not improved.

Her soft brown eyes filled with tears. This young woman could easily have won a prize in anyone's beauty contest, but besides being lovely to look at, she had a will to please her Lord. "I've kept my journal as well as I can, and I think I've learned to tell myself the truth," she said. "But I slipped again. I slip nearly as often as ever. I just don't know what's wrong. I'm more miserable than ever about my sexual behavior."

"Greta, tell me what happened."

"It's what always happens. Last night, my new boy-friend wanted sex. I tried to tell him I couldn't get involved that way, but he wouldn't listen. He kissed me in a way that kept me from saying much of anything, and meanwhile his hands were under my clothes. Without my really agreeing at all, we were into making love. I just don't seem to be able to handle men."

I thought I knew what stood between her and success. "Maybe you need to work at something more than telling yourself the truth. Perhaps now you need to learn to tell your boyfriends the truth in ways they'll grasp more readily than they listen to words."

In effect, over a period of time, I taught Greta how to prevent her own victimization in date rape, and how to play a new role in the drama of heterosexual, interpersonal relationships. In this new role, she would be assertive instead of passive, and would exercise control over her own body rather than yield control to others who had no interest in her wish for purity.

When I asked her where she wanted to draw the boundaries, she quickly replied, "I don't mind holding hands, hugging, or kissing guys I like well enough to go out with, but I think I start losing it when the kissing gets wet and their hands fondle my breasts or genitals."

"Then the first thing you must do is etch that boundary clearly in your own mind," I suggested. "Most people haven't fixed for themselves a clear line beyond which they will not go or allow others to go, and as a result, they don't even realize things have gone too far until it's over. Fix your boundary in your mind before you ever get physically close to someone."

Then I asked her to close her eyes and imagine herself with an attractive man—alone, perhaps, in her apartment. She liked him very much and he liked her. She was to see them side by side on the couch, his arm around her, feeling close and good. "Now he pulls you toward him and you kiss. It's tender and positive for you. Once again, a kiss, but this time his mouth is open—"

"What do I do then?" she interrupted. "I'm always paralyzed at this point!"

"Let's work it out. What could you think of that you might do to alter the direction things are going?"

"This is where I'm stuck. While I try to think of something, he keeps moving ahead. How about pushing him away and telling him to cut it out or go home?"

"You could do that," I replied.

She frowned. "But if I did that," she said, "he might get upset and never call me again. It seems pretty abrupt!"

"I agree," I answered. "Maybe you'd like to plan something just as effective, but more reassuring to the other person. How about pulling yourself away instead of pushing him? You could even give him an extra hug and squeeze his hand when you do it."

"I could go sit in another chair—not too far away, but not close enough to get physical either." Apparently, she was beginning to see how it could work effectively.

"I think, at this point, you ought to talk to him, Greta. Interpret what you're doing and what it means," I suggested.

"Well, how about if I say, 'I need to talk to you!'? I think I should try to stay close to him even if I've moved to another chair. So I could lean forward, even take his hand, and then tell him what I'm trying to do."

"Sure," I replied. "You could say something like, 'I really like you a lot. And I want to see you and express affection, too. But I don't want to get into heavy petting, and I don't want to go to bed with you or anyone before marriage.' How does that sound?"

"I like it," she responded with enthusiasm.

"Sounds good to me," I said. "I think the part about physically changing locations is especially good. I also like the way you envision giving him signs of reassurance and acceptance. Any man is likely to misinterpret your actions as rejection if you don't take pains to show him that's not what you're up to."

"I'm afraid he's going to think I'm some sort of Goody-Two-Shoes, or something."

"Well, why don't you tell him you're not? Can you come up with something you might say along that line?"

Again, she thought for a moment. "How about, 'It's not that I wouldn't enjoy it, or that I'm so perfect. I'm not. But I'm a Christian. I'm trying to learn to please God in this area of my life, and I know I'm already liking myself better, so I don't want to blow it tonight. I'd really appreciate it if you wouldn't push me, but I want you to know that if you do, I intend to stick by what I'm telling you'?"

I thought she'd come up with an effective response, and suggested she try to memorize her lines. Although this seems artificial, it affords considerable aid to a person who is learning a new behavior. Furthermore, I guessed the new role would make Greta nervous and anxious. We may get nervous when we try new interpersonal tactics. Memorizing the new behavior, though somewhat unnatural, will help reduce the anxiety and increase the likelihood of success.

"Do you know what I'm really worried about?" she asked. "I think about what awful things the guy might say or do. I've never tried this before!"

"For instance, what might he say or do?"

"Well, I don't know. He might get his feelings hurt or get angry. Probably get sarcastic or insulting. Maybe he'd leave. Maybe I'd never hear from him again. I don't know."

"What if he did one or more of those things?"

"I would feel bad about losing him. Maybe I could keep from feeling too bad by telling myself I had done right. I'd be pleasing my Lord even if I wasn't pleasing a human being. And there must be somebody somewhere who wants a woman with principles. I think if I told myself those things, I could handle it if he got mad and dropped me from his list. And I guess I could always remind myself that all the times I gave in haven't

brought me any closer to my goal of a Christian marriage and family."

For Greta, the tactics she had planned worked beau-
tifully. After this session, Greta managed to control her
sexual behavior very well. Her current boyfriend did get
angry and end the relationship. Shortly after that, however, she met a man who was attending her Bible study
group and began dating him. The time came when Greta
had to deal effectively with his sexual overtures. (Even
though he was a Christian, he had not learned self-control in sexual matters.) But his response was positive
and cooperative. He admitted that Greta was right and
found himself more interested in her than ever.

A STRATEGY FOR SEXUAL SELF-CONTROL

Joy, you will recall, had only to alter her self-talk to
bring her sexual behavior under control. But Greta
needed a program which involved more than merely al-
tering her self-talk. So did Brandon, the dentist we discussed at the beginning of this chapter. He and I worked
out a total program which effectively changed his pernicious and destructive habits of sexual involvement
with his patients. More often than not, sexual self-control involves a total program.

Step 1: Begin by following God's instructions (Rom.
8:13): ". . . by the Spirit . . . put to death the deeds of the
body." Follow this word literally. Tell God, "I haven't
been handling my own sexual urges well. I've tried, and
I get defeated over and over again. I want to please you,
Lord. Therefore, Holy Spirit, I'm giving you the author-
ity to put to death the illicit deeds of sin in my life: the
uncontrol, the sinful passions, and the ugly desires."
(Here you are not asking God to put your *sexual desires*
to death, for they are good. You are referring to the re-

bellious desires to use sex in ways contrary to God's will for you.) Then, trust in the Lord and His power to bring it to pass.

Step 2: Do your part. Here are some effective things you can do:

First, face the facts and tell yourself the truth. The fact is that many of your values as a Christian are absolutely opposite from those of the culture and of the world in this matter. There can be no rapprochement.

Go on to examine and work on changing your sexual misbeliefs. Keep your journal, keep track of your own sexual misbeliefs in action, and work on challenging and arguing against them.

Work out the truth for the situations you'll be in ahead of time, even write out and memorize what you're going to tell yourself in the tough situations. Then practice your strategies.

Keep a journal record of what happened, what you did, what you told yourself and how it came out. Record your setbacks as well as your victories. Pray them all through.

Tell yourself the truth about the consequences of engaging in sexual behavior that is not commensurate with your commitment to God. Research suggests that we tend to avoid thinking of the consequences when we want to do something we know is bad for us. We actually force thoughts about the painful end results from our minds so they won't restrain us from doing what we ought not do. (For example, people trying to lose weight may tell themselves how they deserve a goo-blob sundae and how good it will taste, and that they will make up for it by extra exercise. Meanwhile, they carefully keep out of their consciousness the truth about how guilty and fat they'll feel after they've consumed it.)

When you want to engage in some illicit sexual behavior, you conveniently avoid thinking about how rotten you'll feel about yourself when it's over, or about the possible exposure to some pelvic inflammatory disease, perhaps one from which you will die, or about the spiritual blight and separation from God you'll suffer. Instead, you tell yourself that you can't help yourself, that your passions are strong and red-blooded, that God will surely understand since He made you this way, that you are so much in love the behavior must be good, and that something this wonderful couldn't be wrong.

It is important to rehearse telling it like it is. Tell yourself the truth about consequences, focus on how you'll feel and think after the behavior is over or after the partner you're with drops you or severs the relationship or turns to someone else. Focus on the truth about how good you'll feel if you learn to hold yourself in control sexually, how much more you'll like yourself if you manage to gain a victory over temptation and learn to make victory a habit.

Second, control situations and persons you spend time with. Stay out of situations likely to lead to illicit sexual behavior—being alone for long periods in a house or apartment with a potential sex partner, for example. It may sound far-fetched, but I have even known people to take off all their clothes and go to bed with someone, meanwhile telling themselves they would not have sexual intercourse—just sleep together. It should be obvious that self-control in such a situation presents many more difficulties than being together in situations of less intense intimacy. Spend time with other couples, groups, and friends.

You can choose whom you will associate with. If you choose to date persons who do not share Christian faith and values with you, you can expect to encounter numerous misunderstandings (unless you simply suppress your own moral and spiritual principles). In nearly all such cases you will be in constant conflict over sexual matters until you give in and do it the other person's way. Therefore, it makes sense for Christians with self-control difficulties to spend their time with others who take the Christian walk very seriously, in sexual matters too. It is just plain irrational to repeatedly date persons who believe sex with anyone is perfectly fine as long as both people consent and no child is conceived.

Third, get married. This may seem a bold suggestion. And it is inappropriate, of course, for those whom God has called to celibacy. Nevertheless, some people believe they should wait to get married for interminable lengths of time, until they have finished advanced degree programs, amassed large sums of money, or done some other thing they believe they must achieve before marriage. Although in our day it may seem odd to suggest that people marry partly in order to make provision for their sexual needs, in the perspective of human history, it is the *delay* of marriage that is odd. God gave marriage specifically to meet human needs for sexual fulfillment and closeness. If you are deferring marriage for any reason, perhaps you need to reconsider.

For example, you may hold the "Prince Charming misbelief." ("Someday, my prince will come . . ." and so forth.) Tell yourself the truth. There are no perfect spouses—and no Prince Charmings. Just real people. Settle for someone who loves God and loves you and, even though he or she is not perfect, get married. It is a part of God's answer for those with self-control problems. Read St. Paul's discussion of this in 1 Cor. 7:9 *in context.*

Fourth, avoid exposing yourself to pornography. It is not true that one can safely view and audit sexually stimulating literature, music, videotapes, movies and TV shows. Jesus' sobering caution against "looking on a woman to lust after her" applies and is underscored by many research studies demonstrating that exposure to such materials increases the probability of engaging in behavior similar to what is depicted.[2]

It may require an act of the will to remove these devices from your life if you have acquired habits of using them. Brandon, for example, had to destroy piles of lewd magazines to help himself avoid feeding old fantasies. But it is worth doing if you are working to develop sexual self-control. Get rid of pornographic materials, and stay away from stores peddling them. Substitute materials which appeal to your other interests and occupy your mind with them. First and foremost, set your mind on the praise of God.

Fifth, stop illicit sexual fantasizing. Again, call to mind the teaching of Jesus that lust is adultery. This teaching, too, has been echoed by results of some psychological research suggesting that much illicit and deviant sexual behavior originates with fantasizing. Masturbation fantasies, in particular, seem to amount to strongly reinforced mental practice of illicit behavior, increasing the likelihood of engaging in that behavior.

It is a misbelief that fantasies cannot be controlled. You can voluntarily change your mental imagery and you can voluntarily stop picturing yourself engaging in behavior you know displeases God.

WHEN THE GOING GETS TOUGH

Russ had been working on gaining control over his habit of meeting and having casual sex with other men in the rest-room of a certain department store. Although

---

[2]The research I have in mind deals with aggressive behavior. Results suggest that when people watch others receive rewards for aggressive actions, members of the audience are thenceforth more likely than before to perform aggressive actions themselves. Reference: Bandura, *op. cit.*

he had done pretty well for three months, he had slipped, and was now feeling pangs of remorse.

"I quit!" he shouted, his face contorted in a look of disgust. "I've tried and tried, and I can't do it."

Russ's reaction to his slip was typical. People trying to gain control over any habitual behavior (such as overeating, alcohol/drug abuse, smoking, temper tantrums) nearly always engage, after a slip, in untruthful self-talk. This set of cognitions tends to make them give up and give in totally to the bad behavior. Nearly always, people in Russ's situation tell themselves the things Russ was now believing and thinking:

- "I obviously can't make it. It's just not in me. I don't have what it takes. Maybe others do, but I don't. I'm somehow defective. I lack the willpower. I'm hopeless."

- "One slip means failure. I have 'fallen off the wagon,' or 'blown my program,' or 'shot myself down.' It shows all my efforts have meant nothing. It means I have ruined everything. I am no longer sexually straight (or, with regard to other behaviors, I'm no longer a successful dieter, I'm no longer a nonsmoker, nondrinker, nonuser, etc.). I'm right back where I started. If I'm not 100 percent successful, I'm a failure. I blew my success record; therefore I'm finished."

- "I'm off the program now. I might as well give up. I quit. I've proved I'm a failure and there's no use trying, so I might as well see myself as I am—a miserable flop. I might just as well go back to engaging in the bad behavior regularly, like I did before, since it does no good for me to try to quit."

If you've ever tried to give up something habitual, you've doubtless indulged some of these misbeliefs. You can probably identify.

Arm yourself in advance for this onslaught of destructive self-talk. It will flood your mind if you happen to slip while you're working on change. Prepare ahead of time, so that, if you do slip you'll be ready to tell yourself the truth and to challenge and defeat these misbeliefs.

See if you can identify the following as truthful:

- One episode or two or three doesn't prove you *can't* quit, just that you *haven't* quit yet. Look at the good record you had until the slip. You had what it took to quit for that length of time. You can do it again. So get right back on your program and learn from your mistakes how to prevent future slips. And quit telling yourself you're hopeless. You know will-power isn't something in your genes, or a fluid in your "willpower tank." It's telling yourself the truth. Do that right now and you'll get back on your program and learn from your slip.

- One slip does *not* mean a failure. That's what the enemy wants you to think. You haven't failed until you stop trying. Stop telling yourself you've done something irreversible. You've had a slip, that's all. It can be an important occasion for self-examination. Instead of calling yourself a failure, study the slip, note how you got yourself lined up for it. And carefully plan how to avoid it in the future. This time you *can* succeed.

Not only Russ, but Brandon, Greta, and many others working on self-control had to learn to handle slips. Many people fall victim to slips, give up trying, and see themselves as helpless losers. Those who learn how to turn slips into educational experiences can go on to pursue their programs with increased success.

A FINAL WORD

If you haven't found your own story in this chapter, you can still apply its principles. There are so many varieties of sexual dyscontrol it would be impossible to discuss them all.

Nevertheless, for most of them, the program presented will be effective. You can use it to gain control now over whatever elements of your sexual behavior seem to be controlling you!

SEVEN

Self-Control and Our Daily Bread

Anne forced herself to chuckle when her four-year-old nephew Tommy pointed his little index finger at her and said, loudly, "Look, Mom, how thick Aunty Anne has gotten!"

But she didn't *feel* like chuckling.

She was already painfully conscious of the weight she'd put on since last Thanksgiving. Forty pounds, at least, had simply grown like a crop of weeds pushing their way up over an unattended garden. If only she could *melt* the fat away. Or prune it off the way she pruned her shrubs. If only she could wake up some morning forty pounds lighter than when she went to bed.

"IF ONLY ..."

"If only ..." Those were Anne's favorite words. They came to mind quite often, carrying a twofold meaning for her: (1) It would be nice if you could lose forty pounds (2) but of course you can't.

Whenever you catch yourself thinking, "If only ...," you might check your meaning. Chances are that you, too, are saying that something would be nice but is impossible.

"If only I could fly ..."

"If only I could meet an enchanted prince!"

"If only I could win a million dollars in a contest!"

Like Anne, many people include, "If only I could lose this superfluous weight!" And, like Anne, they believe there is nothing they can do to rid themselves of excess fat, though getting rid of it would thrill them beyond the power of words to express.

Anne looked longingly at the latest diets featured in her women's magazines, pictured herself looking slim and attractive in a bathing suit, and proceeded to tell herself, in the words of a misbelief we have encountered throughout this book, "I can't!" This way, she prevented herself from trying. We have seen how, in every self-control situation, those two words rob people of willpower and self-discipline by convincing them that effort is useless. So, believing they cannot succeed, they never try—or they try half-heartedly and quit at the first excuse. What a potent misbelief! All by itself, it's sure to keep you fat. Once the devil succeeds in convincing a person that it's impossible to lose weight and keep it off, he has gained control over that person's eating behavior.

"If only . . ." is just another way of convincing yourself of your own sincerity while you go ahead and stuff: "I wish I could, but, alas, I can't." Literally, such words are nonsense. As we've noted in relation to other behaviors, all the actions involved in eating are voluntary actions that cannot be executed by us unless we decide to perform them.

For Christians, the words *I can't* make even less sense, since Christians are empowered as others are not. God has given us His Spirit to energize and direct our behavior. With this power, believers have walked on water, faced lions, conquered kingdoms for the gospel, healed the sick and even raised the dead. When God reveals something as His will for you, put the words *I can't* out of your vocabulary. They are a lie.

Anne would often dream of succeeding. "If only I could lose this excess weight! . . ." she would muse. You, too?

The fact is, *you can—because you can do all things through Christ!*

Before you try, you must believe this, because it must be done by faith. You must believe that Jesus Christ died for you on the cross, that He took away your sins, and therefore nothing stands between you and God's Holy Spirit. Believe that, for the sake of Jesus, God forgives your sins and fills you with mighty power to conquer sin and death and to overcome every misbelief the Enemy has sowed in your heart. *This includes the misbeliefs which cause you to overeat and underexercise.* So stop muttering to yourself, "If only I could control my eating. Stop telling yourself *I can't* and start now to tell yourself *I can lose weight and keep it off because I can count on the power of God.*

VARIATIONS ON A THEME

> **Overeaters' Misbelief #1:** *"I can't lose weight."*

The "I can't" misbelief is one of the most powerful preventors of progress known to man. In obesity, it has many variations. Anne often thought:

> *"I can't lose weight because my body won't co-operate. I was born to be fat, and that's all there is to it."*

It's true that some obese people have larger fat cells than other people, so they have more "storage space" for fat. It's also true that obese people sometimes have more circulating insulin in their blood, so they convert food to fat faster and get hungrier sooner than thin people.

But before you conclude that you were fated to be fat by God himself (a sort of predestination to obesity), or that the way your body was constructed simply *forces* you to be overweight, consider this truth:

> *It is not primarily your body's fat cells or insulin production, but your eating and exercise habits which govern your weight. No matter how many fat cells you have, and no matter how fast you get hungry, nothing causes* you to overeat and underexercise except your own decisions made in view of the misbeliefs you rehearse to yourself.

Here is another version of the "I can't" misbelief:

"I can't be thin because I don't have enough willpower. I can't make myself eat and exercise properly. And I just can't help it that I can't."

If you had to spin straw into gold in order to maintain proper weight, you could truthfully say, "I can't because I don't have what it takes." But ridding your body of excess fat isn't anything like spinning straw into gold, because if you are a follower of Jesus, you already have everything it takes. Willpower is not a substance you either have or don't have. It is truth in your inward parts. It's the habit of telling yourself, among other things, "I *can* develop appropriate eating habits because I belong to Jesus Christ and I can do all things through Him."

Here's another "I can't." Clinicians hear it often, not only from overeaters, but from abusers of drugs, alcohol, tobacco, and other substances. They sink their own ships by convincing themselves of this:

"I can't quit abusing food (or something else) because I have this awful spouse (or terrible relationship or miserable boss or troublemaking friend) driving me to it."

Harvey was a grocer. His weight (close to 400 pounds) nearly disabled him. Harvey believed he had to stuff himself for comfort, because communication with his sick wife was so very difficult and caring for her in her illness was so harrowing. Several times in the day (between meals), Harvey would seek solace in a box of crackers and a quarter pound of cheese, or a can or two of sardines with half a loaf of bread. Few find themselves in Harvey's plight, but many will recognize the misbelief which kept Harvey from changing his habits: *I can't change because some life situation drives me to eat for comfort. X or Y or Z makes me do it!*

Unfortunately, Harvey would not listen to anyone, even his physician, who told him he would soon die if he did not change. Nonetheless, the truth for Harvey was the same as it is for you. No life situation, no matter how difficult, *requires* people to eat (or drink or smoke or take drugs) for comfort. Witness the countless human beings who get through all manner of difficulty *without* abusing food or any other substance. Clearly, difficult circumstances do not force you to seek consolation in food. To make progress against harmful eating habits, you must take up this truth and wield it like a sword against the demonic lie that something in your life forces you to abuse food.

THE OVEREATER'S HANDBOOK OF MISBELIEFS

Most people who struggle with obesity keep a regular catalogue of misbeliefs with which they effectively prevent themselves from progress. They have convinced themselves that what they need is a new diet, or a different metabolism, or a new invention (food without calories!), and until they find it, they're stuck with their burden.

Here is another of the most popular items in the catalogue of overeaters' misbeliefs:

> **Overeaters' Misbelief #2:** *There's got to be an easy way, and until I find it, I'm not about to torture myself losing weight. A person must find an effortless way to do it or not do it at all!*

Hal, a capable, brilliant and paunchy attorney in his late thirties, sought treatment for his depression. Some of Hal's despair was related to his lifelong corpulence. For a long time, Hal had simply refused to go through the difficulties involved in dieting. He told everyone he was not going to put out all that effort. He believed he was taking the "easy" way, eating all he wanted to and enjoying it.

But Hal did not enjoy the smirks he saw on the faces of others when he appeared in a pair of swimming trunks. He did not enjoy panting and puffing on the stairs. He did not enjoy looking at himself in the mirror. He did not enjoy the way attractive young women moved away from him toward the hard, muscular types at parties.

The "easy way" misbelief is everywhere. What do you think is the major selling point of every new fad diet? "It's an *easy* way to lose weight," the book cover promises you. And why do you buy the book? Because you think it would be so easy to lose weight if you could, as the fad diet promises, eat nothing but eggs or grapefruit for three weeks and drop fifty pounds, or have all the meat, fish, and cheese you want and lose weight forever, or eat all you want to of everything as long as you hold one eye closed, or take special fat solvent pills, or drink vinegar, or take deep breaths, or chew your food longer.

To the sorrow of many, the fad diet usually does not work as promised. It causes weight loss, to be sure, but it isn't easy. So, disappointed, you quit, only to fall prey to the next fad diet you see advertised. Meanwhile, you never change your routines, never develop wholesome daily eating habits.

The truth is, *there is no easy way to lose weight.* Weight loss happens only as a result of eating less than you want to eat and exercising more than most people want to exercise. For the person who has not practiced self-discipline before, the habit change required is very difficult indeed. No matter which diet plan you choose, it will demand unpleasant, painful effort. Even with the empowering of the Holy Spirit, progress in this venture means putting up with discomfort and deprivation.

Unless the person setting out to lose weight tirelessly tells himself this truth, he will return to the old misbelief that losing weight is too hard and too demanding. Repeating this stuff to himself, he will scuttle his program and eat uncontrollably. Meanwhile, he will bide his time, waiting for someone to invent the truly painless, truly effortless weight-loss diet.

One of the most influential misbeliefs is one we can call *the "slip" misbelief.* Here it is:

Overeaters' Misbelief #3: *"Since I've slipped off my program and eaten too much of something that isn't good for me, I've failed, blown it, and ruined my plan, so I might as well forget it and pig out. Another proof that I'm just a flop, I can't win, and I may as well quit."*

Some readers will see themselves in the example of Jerry, the psychiatrist, who, at 5'11" and 295 lbs., described himself as "a bit endomorphic." Others, I'm afraid, thought of him as just plain fat. Jerry had a long-standing habit of consoling himself with food. If he got upset in an encounter with a particularly difficult patient, Jerry would likely go out for a piece of pie, or a couple of scoops of chocolate chip ice cream to assuage his uncomfortable tension. In fact, Jerry used food much as some of his patients used tranquilizers.

In counseling, we had made some progress. By forcing himself to battle some of his most deeply ingrained misbeliefs about eating, Jerry had begun to alter some of his fat-producing habits and had kept up a good exercise program, running faithfully three times a week.

Then life bore down on Jerry. One of his patients killed herself after he decided to discharge her from the hospital. Jerry blamed himself for poor judgment. The very same day, his associate with whom he shared an office told Jerry he would be moving into another professional association, so Jerry would have to find someone else to share the rent. On top of that, at about the same time, Jerry's wife, Pat, told him her physician had decided to biopsy one of her breasts, and Jerry felt in the pit of his own stomach some of Pat's fear and tension.

Two days later, Jerry and Pat attended a reception for a retiring colleague, a buffet dinner featuring an incredible dessert called *chocolate decadence*! Jerry told himself as much truth as he could readily call to mind, but very early in the evening he gave up the effort. He was starving emotionally, he told himself, and the gooey chocolate concoction would make him feel a little better—maybe a *lot* better. At last, Jerry gave up and helped himself to a tiny piece of the tempting, butter-creamy chocolate diet-killer. Surreptitiously, Jerry licked every dark thick smudge off his plate.

But the moment he put his fork down, his self-talk turned to accusation: "You blew it! You've done it now. You ruin every program you try. Face it, freak, you're going to be fat forever. And now that you're off the wagon, you might as well go ahead and make a good job of it. Drown yourself in that dark deadly stuff—it makes no difference—you'll always be a fat failure."

"So," Jerry bitterly told me later, "I did have a second piece—and another—and a fourth. Until I couldn't stomach another mouthful. And why not? I'm beat. I came to tell you what happened and why I won't be back to work on my program anymore."

Immediately, I called his attention to the words he was using: beat, failure, glutton, sinful. "You can label it with all those devastating names if you want to," I replied, "but I call it a 'slip.' Nearly everyone has them. And it's critical to tell yourself the truth about a 'slip.' The truth is, you didn't 'fall off the wagon' or 'blow it' or 'wreck a program.' You merely ate too much."

"You mean you don't think I deserve an *F* for failure?"

"Not unless you insist on giving it to yourself. Instead of telling yourself, 'It's all over now! I blew it so badly I might as well admit I'm finished and throw in the towel,' why not get right back to your diet?"

"You make it sound so logical!" Jerry fired back at me. "But I know myself, and I know I'm always this way. I'll succeed at taking off weight for awhile. But sooner or later, I invariably lose control to some sweet, creamy, too-good-to-resist temptation. Then I gain back all I lost and a little more. Your ideas make sense, but I've totalled myself out."

"You know, Jerry," I observed, "you just repeated aloud a misbelief would-be weight-losers bug themselves with regularly."

"And what would that be?" he asked cautiously.

"You grind yourself down endlessly telling yourself one slip is the same as complete failure!"

"Well, isn't it?"

"Of course not. You don't have to turn a bad episode into a catastrophe. Tell yourself, 'I did slip. I didn't really want to eat that chocolate sludge, but I did. That doesn't mean I have to call my whole program a failure. I've eaten exactly the way I had planned to for two weeks, and I'm not about to quit now just because I had a slip. Instead, I'm going right back on my program, and the sooner the better. I won't let one slip convince me that the program is down the drain, and then go ahead and eat all my pounds back on. Instead, I'm going to think over what happened so I can learn from my mistakes and avoid slips in the future.' "

"I guess you're right," Jerry admitted, looking thoughtful. "In fact, I wonder if I haven't been telling myself I've failed as a rationalization, so I could turn back to the easy road I was on before I started all this. I'm going back on my program right now. And I'm going to give a lot of thought to what I can remember about how I let myself slip in the first place."

Jerry learned from his slip to watch himself most carefully when events combined to raise his stress level as they had in the days leading up to this slip. He also learned to recognize the self-talk he had used to enable himself to depart from his program. And he saw clearly that eating to feel better actually made him feel worse in the long run.

"I'M AWFUL"

Negative self-appraisals kept Grace eating. She couldn't believe it! What she'd always thought was that she could rid herself of her bad behavior by beating herself up verbally. She would say, when she had eaten something she shouldn't, "I'm such a terrible pig!" She believed sincerely that making herself feel rotten and evil would constitute self-punishment and would prevent her from repeating the blunder.

"Grace," I insisted, after hearing her technique, "telling yourself what a terrible pig you are will only result in more maladaptive behavior!"

"But I *am* terrible," she replied, sure of her ground. "And I certainly am a pig for eating that super sundae I had yesterday! I wrecked my diet! That's being a pig, in my book."

"Has calling yourself atrocious names caused you to improve your behavior?"

She hesitated, knit her brow in thought for a moment, and replied slowly, "We-e-ell, no, not really, I guess. Doesn't seem to help much."

"That's because making yourself believe you are an unspeakable slob only results, quite logically, in your acting like an unspeakable slob. If I'm right, your negative self-labeling helps produce negative behavior to fit the labels."

A sarcastic smile curled her lips. "So, I'm supposed to tell myself I'm just wonderful when I stuff down 400 calories of superfluous glop!"

"No," I answered. "But I suggest that you *stop* telling yourself that you are an awful something-or-other, and start telling yourself the simple truth, namely, that the thing you ate was attractive. Apricot-walnut pie makes everybody drool!"

"What's the value in telling myself that?" she demanded.

"It's truthful, for one thing. And it can be the start of a realistic appraisal of the actual reasons why you had a slip. Calling yourself names can never help you to analyze a slip with a view toward prevention. But recognizing problem foods and making contingency plans can help."

Grace had taught herself to hold firmly to this lie:

> **Overeaters' Misbelief #4:** *"If I call myself names and beat myself up when I slip, it will help me to not overeat."*

If you, like Grace, beat yourself up with labels when you have a slip, start substituting realistic analysis with a view toward prevention.

"IT'S DREADFUL HOW HUNGRY I FEEL!"

Jack believed that hunger was bad for him. So when he tried to lose weight and felt some hunger pangs, his self-talk reflected beliefs he had learned from his mother—a woman who believed that food and a full belly were most of what it took to live the good life. Jack would tell himself: "How hungry I am! I can just imagine the hydrochloric acid digesting my stomach and eating holes in it. It's terrible to be so hungry and empty inside."

Coming to realize that his notions about hunger were mostly false, and that, for a person working to lose weight, hunger was a wonderful sign of progress, Jack learned to tell himself, "I'm hungry, and that's great. Hunger pangs are good. They signal that my body is consuming its own excess fat—just what I want to happen. I like hunger pangs."

"I'M STARVING FOR SOME CHEESECAKE"

When Sam found himself in a situation where everyone else was eating cheesecake, he would say to himself, "I'm starving for some of that stuff. It looks so good. I can't resist." Sam learned to say instead, "I don't have to have cheesecake right now. Especially since I know I can always have some later. I can go out and buy a cheesecake if I want to tomorrow, or next week, or next month. Right now, I can stop telling myself I have to eat some and that I'll die if I don't."

THE CATALOGUE OF MISBELIEFS GOES ON AND ON

The following are more misbeliefs commonly found in the heads of people trying to improve their eating and exercise habits for weight control. The list could be longer, but I think you'll get the idea. Try to counter each one by devising a truthful response as you read the list. Practice telling yourself the truth in reply to your own favorite misbeliefs about eating behavior.

- The way to be happy is to enjoy yourself. You only live once, you know, and you won't enjoy your life at all if you're always forcing yourself to work on something. Have fun. Doing what you feel like doing is the ticket to the good life.

- It's better not to let myself think about the undesirable and destructive consequences of overeating. Forget the future. It might not come anyway. If you're always thinking about negative things, you'll never have a happy moment. Don't let yourself dwell on the way you look, the tight clothes, the shortness of breath, the difficulty you have climbing stairs, the excess load you put on your heart.

- I haven't lost a pound for three days now, in spite of all my efforts, so I might as well forget the program and eat whatever I like. No sense working on something doomed to fail anyway. I'm probably just not made to be thin.

- Since it's of crucial importance to feel better rapidly and not to stay upset, I should eat something when I'm unhappy to help myself feel better right away. Food is consolation. Eating is relaxation. It must be bad for you to be so tense, so have a bite to eat—a piece of pie, maybe?

- I know people who eat all they want to without gaining weight. It's unfair for me to have to control my eating when they don't have to pay any attention at all to theirs. If things were fair and just I wouldn't be fat, but they aren't and I am, so I might as well face the fact that *for me* it would be difficult to be thin. It wouldn't be worth it. It's easy for other people, but I just get a raw deal from life.

- I'll eat it now and make up for the extra calories by cutting back tomorrow. I can always eat less tomor-

row or skip breakfast the next day. It'll be just as if
these calories don't count at all.

- I've stuck to my program all week and I owe myself
a reward—I'm going to have something sweet and
sticky! I've been good, I've got a little fun coming. I
actually have been hard on myself. I deserve something nice.

- It's been a terrible week and I need something
good—I'm going to treat myself and go off my program, just for tonight. Nobody could stand what I've
put up with. Who could blame me for having a treat?
I don't always go through the mill like I have this
week. So tonight's an exception.

- This dieting and exercising—it's too hard. It's awful!
I haven't done anything to deserve such misery. Poor
me.

- I need it, I have to have it, I can't live without it, so
I'm certainly entitled to eat it. You can't deny your
needs or you'll warp your personality.

- I hate myself! I'm such a fat, ugly failure and loser,
I'll never be any better. I might as well go ahead and
eat lots. What difference does it make anyway? A
failure might as well fail.

- Nobody cares about me; nobody really cares
whether I gain or lose, so I might as well eat and
gain weight—it won't matter to a single soul. Since
nobody loves me, what I do makes no difference at
all! So I'll stuff myself.

Remember, the reason for paying such close attention
to your beliefs, the ideas running through your mind, and
the assumptions you hold so certain you don't even bother
to think them over is that beliefs occasion behavior. That
is, we act according to what we believe.

Even if you *think* you believe all the right things about
eating, if, when the chips are down, your eating behavior
leads to bad consequences for you, it's important to ask

yourself what you *really* believe—especially at the moment of temptation. If you do, you will discover the misbeliefs governing your unadaptive behavior. And you can begin to work on replacing them with the truth.

GETTING CONTROL OF YOUR EATING BEHAVIOR

Now we're ready to develop a simple plan for gaining control of your eating behavior. Let's take it step by step. As you have learned during your reading of the previous chapters, you will need to keep a journal.

Step 1: Set clear, realistic goals for yourself. Write your goals out in your journal and write them in specific, clear, concrete language, so you will be able to tell when you have achieved them: *Not,* "I want to lose weight," *but,* "I want to lose nine pounds over the next four weeks." *Not,* "I want to cut down on sweets," *but,* "I won't put sugar in my tea." *Not,* "I hope I can eat less," *but,* "I won't have any snacks between meals." *Not,* "I'm going to try to tell myself the truth more," *but,* "I'm going to locate the misbeliefs that lead me to eat maladaptively, write them down, and work on finding and substituting the truth in their place."

Step 2: Log all foods eaten each day. Log for just one week first, keeping track of when, where, and with what accompanying activities and feeling the food was consumed. Don't try to change anything yet. When you have a record of one week's eating, decide what changes you want to make and add them to your list of goals.

In the second week, record foods as you did the first week. This time, monitor your self-talk at times when you eat too much of the wrong things. Write down all misbeliefs, all inaccurate self-talk related to such eating. Work on finding the truth and write that out to replace the negative and misbelieving statements. Work on replacing the wrong self-talk with your new truths in daily life. Keep this up until your goal is reached.

DEALING WITH PROBLEMS

Almost nothing worthwhile is easy. And that applies to making changes in behaviors as personal as eating. Here are some of the common problems encountered by others. You should be sure to log problems you encounter along the way and record what you did about them.

The problem of the party. Most people plan their programs without remembering that they will probably not have all their meals in a situation they can control. They will be invited to gatherings where food is served for refreshment, to dinner parties, and to restaurants or soda fountains.

First, pray for the operation of the spiritual fruit of self-control in the anticipated situation. Then, in the presence of God, believing He wants you to exercise self-control, make a plan. It is imperative to plan in advance how you are going to cope with the pecan pie, the caramel creme, the fresh bread, or the chocolate mousse. When you're going to a restaurant, plan in advance what foods you'll order and how you'll handle the "dessert tray" brought around to tempt you.

Write out your planned strategy. Then rehearse it in your imagination several times. Picture yourself at the party, envision the pecan pie with gobs of whipped cream on it, and rehearse telling yourself something like, "I don't need that pie, attractive as it is. I can always get pecan pie at another time. Tomorrow or next month, if I like. For now, I can do without it and have a cup of coffee instead." See yourself passing up the pie and imagine the sense of accomplishment you will feel after the temptation has passed. Imagine God saying to you: "Well done!"

The problem of the hurt hostess: "Oh, but Merilee, I made that dessert just for you, because I know how much you like it. Surely you're going to have some, aren't you?" Most of us are sitting ducks for this kind of onslaught against our program.

As I discussed this problem (which nearly everyone will encounter) with one client, she asked, "How can I refuse to eat something when it will hurt someone's feelings?"

Maybe this is a stumbling block for you, too. Tell yourself the real facts: The hostess will survive if you don't indulge in the special dessert created "just for you." Christian love does not mean that you must throw away the gains you're making in self-control, the gains God himself has taught you to make, merely in order to prevent someone from getting upset.

Tell yourself and your hostess the truth—namely, that having a piece would really set you back, and that while it looks terrific and you'd like nothing better, you're going to force yourself to pass it up. Tell her how much you appreciate her thoughtfulness. You must rehearse this interaction in advance, imagining yourself doing it just the way you plan to. The reason for advance covert rehearsal is that this is (probably) new behavior for you, and anything new is difficult to bring off without practice. With practice, it becomes more likely you'll pass up the rich dessert and come through the persuasive pressuring of your hostess with flying colors.

The problem of eating to reduce tension: Some people have learned to reach for food as a tranquilizer when they are feeling strong emotion or tension due to stressors. When life becomes stormy, they look for relief and solace in a couple of sandwiches or a box of cookies. If that is your current strategy, you will need to give some thought to planning alternatives.

Learn deep muscle relaxation (noting the cautions mentioned earlier). When you are emotionally overwrought or tense, use your relaxation skills to reduce the discomfort and the anxious feelings. Consciously substitute relaxation for eating as a means of feeling better. Learn to locate the self-talk in your internal monologue and find the misbeliefs you are regaling yourself with to make yourself tense. Replace them with the truth. Learn to deal directly with people whose behavior upsets you when this is appropriate, rather than trying to handle the problem by putting on another layer of fat.

OTHER PROBLEMS YOU MIGHT HAVE TO DEAL WITH

You must plan in advance for such situations as the following. They come up sooner or later.

- You're out with a group from church after a meeting. Everybody orders copious amounts of food and you know the check will be evenly divided so you'll have to pay for theirs if you don't eat as much as they do. You don't want to make a fuss or attract attention to the fact that you are trying to cut down your food intake. What can you do?
- You're on a vacation, the food is great, and you've already paid for all of it, even what you don't eat.
- Other people tell you, "You're starving yourself! You should eat. It won't hurt you. C'mon, be a sport. You're a party wrecker." You feel a strong urge to give in and eat just to get them off your back.
- You have a mate who doesn't support you at all, and keeps zapping you for your efforts at learning self-control (probably from envy and fear that you'll succeed and exhibit more self-control than they are capable of).
- You're so hungry you could eat grass. Starving, absolutely starving!

Most people who get up the courage to begin a program of eating control do not think in advance about how they will handle these and other situations where the strong environmental pressure brings on a slip. It is imperative to come before God in prayer for victory in such situations. Anticipate them. Foreseeing they are likely to arise, invent a response to each of them. Devise what you will say and what you will do. *Then rehearse the situation in your mind several times over, imagining yourself gaining victory over the temptation, and feeling a sense of accomplishment in the Lord, a sense of having done well in His strength and power.*

EXERCISE

Have you ever heard of a *set-point*?

According to some physiologists, your body controls weight, in part, by maintaining and defending weight at a certain level called a *set-point*. It's as if you have a built-in "weight-o-stat" (something like a thermostat for heat control), programming your body to keep your weight right where it is. Most dieters have discovered this mechanism when they've hit a plateau and found themselves hard pressed to lose any more weight for a while, regardless of strict adherence to a good program.

It is believed that aerobic exercise, regularly practiced, can alter metabolism enough to lower your body's *set-point*. With its set-point lowered, your body assists you in your efforts to develop self-control and keep your weight at an appropriate level. Even if you overeat on one or another occasion, your body will rapidly return your weight to the level marked by your lowered *set-point*. Other values in aerobic exercise for control over eating: it burns calories at a much higher rate than sedentary activities do; some authorities believe it reduces appetite. Most people assume exercise increases appetite, but apparently the opposite is true. It reduces tension, depression, and anxiety very effectively (another substitute for the habit of eating to overcome tension). Running, swimming, jogging, bike riding, rowing, and walking are examples of activities with aerobic value.

It must be stressed that such exercises are probably worse than useless when indulged in only occasionally or sporadically. A program of regular practice trains the various physical systems and delivers the above-listed benefits. See that you give yourself a minimum of three or four exercise periods per week. Each session should involve about thirty minutes of activity sufficient to keep your pulse elevated.

Consult an appropriate source for appropriate pulse rates for various ages and other detailed information on exercise. A manual of instructions for exercise is available from the American Heart Association.[1] People who are physically ill, accustomed to an extremely sedentary lifestyle, or above the age of forty should consult a physician before beginning a serious exercise program.

ANOREXIA

Unfortunately, the caution with which I am going to close this chapter must be based on unproved assumptions. Nevertheless, I am going to include it for those few individuals who seem unwilling to do anything without going overboard.

Although the cause of *anorexia nervosa* (literally, *lack of appetite due to nerves*) is not known, it is conjectured by some experts that the disease may be due to excessive dieting and overconcern about weight. It is true that victims of anorexia exhibit a morbid and pathological desire to lose weight. That is their cardinal psychological symptom. Even though many of them are emaciated from self-starvation to the point of having lost nearly all their body fat and a good deal of their muscle tissue, anorexics typically insist that they *must* lose five or ten pounds more.

---

[1]Lenore Zohman, M.D., *Exercise Your Way to Fitness and Heart Health,* 1974.

If they do, they will then want to lose five pounds in addition. And if nothing happens to halt the process, these poor victims will starve and exercise themselves to death.

Development of self-control works in two directions. If you need to develop self-control to decrease the amount of food you consume, the material in this chapter will work for you. If, however, you find yourself wanting to go further than the weight levels suggested by health authorities, if you have turned weight-loss into an end-in-itself, if you hear others commenting that you have gone too far, are too thin, or are beginning to appear emaciated, you need to develop self-control over your deadly desire to worship thinness as your false god.

Victims of this disease tell themselves gross lies. At some point in the progress of the illness, probably due to physiologically determined symptoms of starvation, these people lose their ability to distinguish truth from untruth regarding their weight. Then they must have help. If you suspect that you may be in this group, or if someone you know and care for appears to you to be a victim, don't try to deal with the problem alone. See a Christian psychologist or physician experienced in the treatment of eating disorders. The sooner professional help is obtained, the better.

"WELL DONE!"

Remember Anne? She learned by accomplishing her God-given goals that her "I can't" was a lie. She could and she did. You can too. No matter how many times you've tried and failed to gain control over your interactions with food (or drugs or alcohol or any other abused substance), you can "do all things through Christ."

But you must *do* the program! Reading about it may make you feel as though you're already controlling your eating. But that's not how it works. You must start your journal, trace and replace your misbeliefs, and walk with

God through the various elements of the program suggested. Then you, too, can succeed—and you, too, can hear your Father saying, "Well done!"

A DIET?

Some will wonder when we come to the part about a magical diet. They cannot imagine controlling their intake without a diet. But you won't read about a diet in this book. You can find plenty of them, probably in your own library, and if not there, in any bookstore or any stack of women's magazines.

Diets don't work. They would all accomplish loss of weight if people followed them, but people cannot follow most of them—not forever. And since most of them don't teach anyone to eat normally, as soon as the diet is abandoned, the person resumes his old and maladaptive out-of-control eating behavior.

Our desire is to learn to eat ordinary foods at ordinary meals like ordinary people who, controlled by the Spirit of God, have learned the spiritual fruit of self-control in relation to their daily bread.

EIGHT

How to Break a Habit

Sometimes we bewail our habits, but, in many ways, daily life wouldn't be possible without them.

What if we had to think through every movement involved in brushing our teeth in the morning? What if, each time, it felt as awkward as if we'd never brushed before? Imagine the care, thought, and energy we'd have to invest just to have clean teeth.

What if we couldn't count on habits when we eat? When we read a book? When we greet people? Answer the phone? Make a call? What about driving? Can you imagine having to think about each movement of your hands and feet every single time you drive the car? Without habits, you'd be too occupied mentally with thinking, willing, and executing each motion to pay attention to anything else. Habit takes over the execution of behaviors so our conscious minds are available for higher and more rewarding pursuits.

BUT, WHAT ABOUT. . . ?

But, what about *bad* habits? What about habits we wish we didn't have? Some habits, once constructive, have outlived their usefulness. Some have never had positive value. Some have always been destructive. What about those habits that are about as welcome as a houseguest who came for a week and stayed for eight months?

What about sleeping through the alarm? or interrupting other people? or smoking cigarettes? or being late every time you go anywhere? or a 500-calorie-a-day ice-cream habit? or avoiding exercise? or gulping five cans of pop a day? or staring at late-night TV shows until the wee hours? or popping tranquilizers? or drinking too much every Saturday? or skipping church services? or sleeping too late for prayer? or. . . ? Well, you can add your own hard-to-break-but-you'd-like-to habits.

No question about it. We need some of these habits like we need higher taxes or pneumonia. Most of us would be better off without nail-biting, snacking on sweets, overdoing coffee and tea, puffing tobacco and driving without seat belts. We could have richer lives if we stopped avoiding Bible reading, prayer, taking our vitamins, visiting friends, and exercising regularly.

Some habits are habits of *o*mission. We are in the habit of *not* doing what our deepest and best selves want to do. Other habits are habits of *com*mission, of automatically doing what our deepest and best selves do *not* want to do. Most people have tried to break bad habits, and have found it's not easy.

One way to summarize this book on self-control might be to say that it's a book about changing habits. Heretofore, we've dealt with specific, commonly found, unwanted habits. Now, before we end our discussion of self-control, it's time to learn some general principles—principles you can apply to changing all sorts of unwanted habitual behavior, principles for learning self-control.

In this chapter you will discover tools for changing even deeply ingrained habits. You can change habits of omission or habits of commission.

WHAT ABOUT WILLPOWER?

I once came across an advertisement for a play by Brook Berry entitled "God's Will, Will's Will, and Will's God." I thought it was a fabulous title. To me, it suggests that a person's will accords with that of the god he serves. In other words, whatever your will actually lines up with is your god. If you really serve the God and Father of the Lord Jesus Christ, your will is to do His will.

I don't think much of the term *willpower*. People rarely use it except as a pseudo-explanation for the other fellow's success in breaking a habit. "He has willpower; I don't," we say to excuse our failures.

Instead of bewailing our lack of willpower (which, of course, we consider God's fault, since He hasn't given us enough of it), we can determine, as Jesus did, that "my food is to do the will of him who sent me" (John 4:34). Jesus was saying that His will wasn't independent or self-determined. His life wasn't based on following a will of His own. Rather, His will was so lined up with that of the Father that His will and the Father's will were united in perfect accord. We can begin to handle any and every bad habit in our lives when we will, with Jesus, to do God's will *all the time*. So, to change a habit, start with a commitment to God: "Father, my deepest desire and will is to do your will." Then when the going gets rough, remind yourself over and over that you really want God's will and only God's will. Because this is true, there is no difference between God's will and your highest will. Whenever the enemy insinuates that anything else is the case, tell yourself the truth: "I want what God wants."

PRAY FOR WISDOM AND BELIEVE GOD GIVES IT

When you will to do God's will, you naturally want to know what God's will is. Knowing and doing God's will the Bible calls *wisdom*.

When you consider attacking an unwanted habit, ask yourself: "Is it God's will for me to break habit X using procedure Y at time T? Or does God have something else for me to do first, reserving the breaking of habit X for another time or another method? Even when you know right and wrong in general, you need *wisdom* when it comes to applying your knowledge to particular instances in your life. Consider this admonition:

> If any of you lacks wisdom, let him ask God who gives to all men generously and without reproaching, and it will be given him. But let him ask in faith, with no doubting, for he who doubts is like a wave of the sea that is driven and tossed by the wind. For that person must not suppose that a double-minded man, unstable in all his ways, will receive anything from the Lord. (James 1:5–9)

Don't overlook the Apostle's insistence on faith. Believe God has answered your prayer for wisdom, so the urge to go to work on the bad habit is directly from God. You can't get anywhere if you vacillate about whether or not God wants change. You must go forward single-mindedly, or you jeopardize your chances of succeeding. "I don't know for sure if I can do it—I don't think I can" is one of the most defeating of misbeliefs when you're working on changing a habit. Believe, on the basis of the promise of God, that He is leading you and enabling you to succeed.

WRITE A PLAN

Once you know God's leading, start a journal. We have seen other examples of journal-keeping in earlier chapters. A journal is an important aid. When you write things down, spell them out, and see them in front of you, they acquire a certain objectivity. No longer is your plan "just an idea in your head." Use your journal to help you remember what it is you have set out to do and how you planned to go about the task. Date your entry, tell what you plan to change, and how you plan to go about it. Make your plan on the basis of the various strategies suggested in this chapter, and list the strategies you will use.

Your first journal entry might look something like this:

January 8.

Prayed for wisdom about lateness. God wants me to stop being late for everything and to arrive on time, or a little bit early. Since He wants me to change my lateness habit, I know I can do it because I can do all things through Him.

Plan:

I will use these strategies:

1. Record my self-talk to determine my lateness misbeliefs. Concentrate on what I tell myself when I know I have to go someplace and be there at a certain time before I start trying to change.

2. Keep notes on what happens when I arrive at places late (to determine what reinforces my continued lateness habit).

3. Keep an accurate record of the times I leave and the times I arrive at places for one week before I try to change.

4. Reinforce myself for arriving early each time I do it. I will allow myself a coke each time I succeed. No cokes unless I do succeed. Also, I will try to think of a way to do away with anything that is now reinforcing me for arriving late.

5. Punish myself every time I am late. I will make myself get up earlier next morning whenever I am late for anything. I will set my alarm 15 minutes earlier for each 5 minutes or portion of 5 minutes I am late.

6. Keep an accurate record of my progress, including notes on leaving and arrival times, reinforcers and punishments, and my self-talk con-

nected with leaving and arriving episodes.

7. Praise and thank God for successes.

MAKE YOUR GOALS CLEAR AND SPECIFIC

Why have you had such rotten results in your efforts to change bad habits? you wonder. Maybe it has something to do with the way you began. Lots of people make no progress because they never tell themselves precisely what it is they plan to change.

Do you make *vague* resolutions like, "become a nicer person," or "learn to be more loving"? Do you tell yourself with a firm squaring of your jaw, "I am going to try to be more punctual" or "I'm determined to start eating a more healthful diet" or "I'm starting tomorrow to become more neat and clean"? You might have made yourself feel good because the words sound so resolute, but you aren't very likely to change anything just because you made some vague vows in a firm tone of voice. Such foggy sentiments often prevent us from thinking clearly enough to take action. We can substitute sentiments for real effort and feel like we're working at change when all we're doing is talking. Although using concrete language might be difficult at first, definite goals are a prerequisite for making headway against bad habits.

Here are some examples of the above resolutions stated as concrete change goals:

- I will stop putting other people down with sarcastic answers to their questions.
- I will make certain I do one thing each day to meet another person's needs.
- I will arrive at the office at five minutes to eight or earlier each morning.
- I will eat red meat no more than three times per week, and I will eat a helping of fresh vegetables at two of my meals each day.

- I will shower and wash my hair before I dress every morning.

Write out your goals as explicitly, clearly, and concretely as you possibly can before you begin working toward change.

TELL SOMEONE ELSE

Long ago, when I was an avid cigarette smoker, I determined to try to quit. "I won't tell anyone," I resolved, "because I might fail and then I would look ridiculous." I was, of course, "making provision for the flesh" (Rom. 13:14). I provided an "out" in case I should find the desire to smoke overwhelming. I was actually planning for the time when I would resume smoking. Not such a hot idea if one really wants to quit.

Paul's instruction in Romans 13:14 continues to be apropos. If you are serious about habit change, do *not* make provision for the flesh. Don't leave yourself an escape hatch. Burn your bridges! There are many ways to apply Paul's words to habit change, but one very good way to block the flesh is to *tell someone else*. I should have told someone, "I've given up smoking cigarettes."

In the Body of Christ, we are joined to one another so we can build one another up, strengthen one another, put one another in mind of the truth, and love one another. When I let a Christian brother or sister know about my projected habit change, I enlist the aid of the Body. The other person can pray for me, admonish me when I need it, reinforce me when I have it coming, and remind me of the truth when I fail to tell it to myself. Moreover, the mere fact that someone else knows serves as a positive force, adding a social dimension to my battle for control over a habit.

PAY ATTENTION TO YOUR MISBELIEFS

Use your journal to record your misbeliefs, the untruthful contents of your internal monologue that spur you on to continue your old, undesirable habits forever. I know it's more fun to forget that junk and to pretend that your mind is full of nothing but Christian verities. I know it's no picnic to write out all that nonsense and to face up to the fact that this clutter still clogs your internal monologue. But if you don't get it out in front of you, on paper, where you can look at it straight-on, it's too easy to ignore it and to miss noticing how your own self-talk facilitates continuing a practice you want to stop.

GET 'EM WHILE THEY'RE HOT

One purpose of journal-keeping is to enable you to catch misbeliefs when they are "doing their thing," when they're "hot." So tune in and start writing in the heat of the battle. "What am I telling myself now? What are my thoughts?" Ask yourself these questions during those moments when you are in conflict about buying a pack of cigarettes or shutting off the alarm for those forty forbidden winks that make you late for work every day? During times of conflict and temptation, capture your self-talk, unpleasant as it may be, and write it in your journal just as soon as you can.

After you've recorded your relevant misbeliefs, debate and argue against them, raise evidence and facts. Keep working until you have convinced yourself of their utter falseness. Replace them with the truth and act on it. Continue until you know you have your behavior under control by the truth which must set free because Jesus said it would.

SOME SAMPLE SELF-CONTROL MISBELIEFS

Throughout this book, I have tried to give you concrete examples of the most common misbeliefs in the heads of people working for self-control over particular behaviors. The reason for including so many actual misbeliefs in these chapters is that they serve as examples of what to look for when you are working on your own self-control problems. These examples, or variations of them, may pop up in your own mind. People with similar problems tend to believe similar errors. Or, you may discover entirely different misbeliefs as you explore what you've been doing to promote your own bondage.

Here are some common notions contributing to the difficulty some people experience with habit change.

- *I can't control this habit.* This is the false belief that other people and circumstances are responsible for your behavior and you yourself are not, because you can't help it.
- *I shouldn't have to do anything hard or experience anything unpleasant in order to change.* This is the erroneous belief that self-control and habit-change are too hard for you, and that it is really easier to avoid responsibilities and tough tasks than to tackle them.
- *My behavior is determined by past events.* This is the misbelief that your history is all-important. Whatever bad habits you have now are a result of mistreatment or mishandling by your parents, teachers, or friends in the past, so there is little or nothing you can do about them.
- *I need someone else to do this for me.* This is the misbelief that your bad habits will be broken only by someone else praying for you, laying hands on you, or counseling you, and that you need merely to sit back and wait passively for change to come. Nowhere in the Bible are we encouraged to substitute someone else's prayers for our own responsible decision-making while we remain uncommitted to anything but pleasure and play.

- *If I want something I should have it. It's a dirty shame if I ever have to control my strong desires.* This is the belief that you have a right to be happy all the time, that no strong wish of yours should remain unfulfilled, and that you should not have to suffer loss or deprivation. You think of all your desires as psychological "needs" which must be fulfilled, or else.

- *I shouldn't have to be kept waiting for anything. If I have to defer gratification, it's terrible.* This is the belief that you ought to get instant results, and not have to go through hard times to arrive at the happiness and joy in store at the end of the road. It should all be yours right now.

- *I can't stand it.* The notion that you can't stand something unpleasant is deeply rooted in human misbelief systems. Many people believe they can't stand anxiety, frustration, mental pain, not sleeping well, or feelings of nervousness. These folks also believe that, because they say they can't stand something, they are entitled to have someone dispense with it for them.

- *I'm so worthless I really don't matter, so I might as well go ahead and keep my bad habit.* This is the belief that you are so ugly, or fat, or dumb, or stupid you can't get any worse. No one cares what happens to you, so why should you? You have no value, so you aren't worth saving from the consequences of your bad habits. (Wrong, wrong, *wrong!*)

These and other misbeliefs that rob people of self-control have some similarity to each other and to misbeliefs spelled out in earlier chapters. That is because they all converge at one point. They all constitute arguments persuading you to go right ahead and practice your undesirable, self-defeating, misery-generating habits.

In previous chapters, you have read the truth countering each misbelief presented. Now, at this stage in your progress toward better self-control, you can seek the truth yourself. For practice, try countering each of the eight misbeliefs above with the truth. Why not write out the truth, just as you will write it in your journal when you actually work on changing a habit.

WANT TO KNOW WHY YOU DO WHAT YOU DON'T WANT TO DO? LOOK AT WHAT FOLLOWS YOUR ACTIONS!

When you want to change a habit, you want to do something different from what you are now doing. So you start trying to change. And the first shock comes when you discover how determined that habit seems to be. It acts as if it has resolved to stick with you. "I didn't know it would be so hard," you grumble. "Why on earth do I keep doing it when I really, deep down, don't want to keep doing it?"

A good question!

And if you pursue it thoughtfully, you may discover something you didn't expect: the answer occurs *after* the behavior occurs. That is, what happens to you as a result of doing a behavior is often the cause of the behavior. Most people look for causes in the past—assuming that whatever causes them to act the way they act must have happened *prior to* the act. (Like, "I put others down and insult them cleverly because I was hurt so much by my father's put-downs when I was a child.") While there may be some validity to that line of thinking, there isn't much you can do about what happened to you long ago.

Sometimes it is more fruitful to ask, "What usually happens *after* my unwanted actions?" Example: "What *follows* when I zap someone with a clever, sarcastic put-down?" Answer: "The other person wilts, bystanders giggle, and I feel powerful and clever."

As B. F. Skinner has taught us so well, if an action is followed immediately by a rewarding consequence, we are more likely to perform that action again. Each rewarded repetition makes the likelihood of repeating it again greater. So when this sequence occurs over and over again, the tendency to repeat it becomes exceedingly strong. We then have a potent habit which may be very resistant to change as long as the rewards keep occurring.

Keep a record in your journal each time you perform your unwanted behavior. And be sure to include a note describing the immediate consequences which could be rewarding to you. Sometimes you can change the consequences or prevent their occurrence and thus remove the rewarding results of the undesirable habit. If you are successful and can actually arrange for elimination of the reward, your habit will weaken and drop away.

For example, suppose you could get your family and friends to learn to stand up to you when you zap with an insult, and to stop chuckling at your "cleverness." Very likely, your habit of putting others down would change rapidly. What if, every time you arrive at work late, instead of smiling and wishing you a "good morning," your associates ignored you for the rest of the day? Would that help you arrive on time or earlier? Probably.

People lighting cigarettes in public places these days are liable to be met with pointed stares, or even polite requests to move or put the cigarette out. Many smokers have already curtailed the amount they smoke because of such consequences.

Consider whether you can think of a way to alter the consequences of your unwanted habitual behavior. Sometimes this tactic is hardly practicable. Sometimes it can be done. If it seems feasible to you, you will have another potent weapon in your battle.

WHAT IS MY CUE?

If you were ever in a play, you had to respond to cues. Did it ever occur to you that your unwanted behavior occurs on cue? You can see, with a moment's thought, that even the toughest habits occur only under certain conditions or in particular circumstances.

For instance, I once knew a pastor who was a golf addict. He played golf much more than he should have. Nevertheless, he didn't practice his swing while he was making pastoral calls or rehearse putting while he was conducting funerals. His golfing behavior occurred only in the presence of appropriate cues, circumstances proper for golf-playing. That is, he waited to execute golfing behaviors until he was on the golf course—which was as often as he could manage, to the irritation of his wife and congregation.

Most people don't smoke in church, whistle in court, or chew their fingernails in front of a job interviewer. Why? Because cues which elicit those behaviors are missing in those situations. So if you can avoid the cue circumstances that elicit your bad habit, you can do one more thing which will help you eliminate it.

As you enter episodes in your journal, be sure to note the cue circumstances in which each episode occurred. You *may* discover that it would be possible to alter or avoid the circumstances which presently serve as cues for your unwanted actions.

If, for example, a cup of coffee is your cue for lighting a cigarette, try eliminating the coffee to help yourself avoid smoking. Suppose you're trying to stop spending two hours every day combing carefully through the newspaper. You'd like to scan the paper and save time. Instead of curling up in your favorite chair, try doing your newspaper reading standing up or in a straightbacked chair with a hard wooden seat and no arms. Removing the comfortable conditions you have associated with poring over each line of the daily *Gazette* will help you save time for other pursuits God may have put on your heart.

You can use cues to initiate new habits, too.

Do you want your child to learn to wipe his feet before he walks on your clean floors with mud on his boots?

You've tried nagging, reminding and threats to no avail. None of those devices will change habits. Try this: put a rubber toy that squeaks under the front doormat. The squeak will serve as a cue for the shoe cleaning, and after a few days, the doormat alone will become a cue for Junior's new behavior. When that happens you can remove the rubber duck.

After you have learned by journal-keeping what typically precedes a habitual action, pray for enlightenment and wisdom. The Lord may show you how you can control the behavior by changing the conditions or cues which elicit it.

BREAK THE CHAIN SOONER

Some habits are the predictable consequences of a series of actions and circumstances, each one linked by habit to the next. So *A* leads to *B* leads to *C* leads to *D* . . . and so on, in a chain until the cue eliciting the unwanted action occurs, after which the undesirable event is practically irresistible. One way of controlling such habits is to break the chain sooner, while you are still firmly in control of your actions.

A young attorney and his wife, both of whom had recently received Jesus as their Savior and Lord, expressed concern over their marital fights.

"Our arguments usually escalate until Cliff loses his temper and yells at me. He's so loud he seems out of control, and I'm afraid of him at those times," said Dotty. Cliff agreed her account was accurate and earnestly recounted his efforts and resolutions to control his temper—all of which had been fruitless.

They kept a journal, recounting the events leading up to every temper tantrum. We discovered a regular chain of events, each leading to the next, until, at the end of the chain, Cliff would blow up. By this time, his emotions were so strong, control was exceedingly difficult.

The couple agreed to break the chain as soon as either one of them became aware of strong negative feelings during discussion of a problem. They decided to go to separate rooms for 15 minutes before resuming their conversation. Temper outbursts became less frequent. Eventually, they were able to work out most of their disagreements without separating, and Cliff's temper appeared to be under excellent control. They felt certain God's Spirit had directed and aided them in developing their new "self-control."

Perhaps the Spirit of Truth will illuminate a chain of events leading up to your unwanted actions. Ask Him for counsel about where and how you can halt progress early in the chain and so gain victory over an unwelcome habit.

REINFORCEMENT

Psychology, in its search for scientific precision, has managed to discover very few principles reliable enough to be called "laws." One of the few real laws in the field of behavior is the so-called *law of reinforcement*. It appears obvious to me that God has built the law of reinforcement into the world He created. We have already learned, earlier in this chapter, to ask ourselves what rewards our bad habits, thus applying the law of reinforcement for better self-understanding. This law, like other scientific laws, describes regularities. It states:

> If a behavior is followed immediately by a rewarding consequence, this raises the probability of that behavior occurring again.

Not only has God programmed the universe so that it rewards us for certain behaviors (picking strawberries, for instance), but He has attached promises of reward to His commandments. According to Scripture, rewards will follow God-pleasing actions. Jesus said, "Every one who has left . . . [everything else] . . . for my name's sake will receive a hundredfold, and inherit eternal life" (Matt. 19:29).

Rewarding behavior repeatedly may produce a habit—and sometimes that will be an unwanted habit. Tina discovered, to her chagrin, that by giving little Lance a cookie to quiet him when he whined, she had actually caused him to whine more regularly. In other words, though the child's complaints stopped when he received the cookie, he learned to complain and whine more often to receive cookies. Whining became a habit.

When Tina realized Lance's whining was a habit she had helped him learn, she was able to do her part to break his habit of whining.

How did she do it? Tina began rewarding Lance for *not* whining. Cookies? Lance now got them *only* when he hadn't whined for a two-hour stretch. Gradually, Tina lengthened this interval.

REWARDING YOURSELF FOR INCOMPATIBLE ACTIONS

Reward yourself for doing actions that make performing your habit impossible. Try to think of behavior incompatible with the habit you want to break. Think of something you can do that makes doing your habit impossible (or at least unlikely).

Harry, as a case in point, was sick and tired of wasting every evening watching mindless TV shows. "But I can't quit" he insisted. "I leave the set off for a while—but an hour or so into the evening I feel like I can't stand it! I give up and switch it on and drift into my customary half-conscious state until bedtime. Meantime, I don't like myself at all."

Harry decided to reinforce himself for doing something incompatible with TV watching. On his three "TV nights" each week Harry took Christian growth classes at his church. He had planned to reward himself for attending class regularly and on time by seeing a movie on Fridays. However, he found the classes so interesting and profitable, they provided enough reward so that he was able to break his TV addiction for good.

Luann and I had worked hard on her melancholy feelings. I, for my part, believed I had done all I could. I had taught her how to discover misbeliefs, the destructive notions she accepted uncritically and repeated over and over to herself. I had showed her with painstaking clarity the truth with which she could replace her misbeliefs and enjoy feeling good again. She seemed to grasp everything I'd taught her and to agree wholeheartedly with every word. But Luann continued to repeat her maladaptive thoughts: "Things are sure to get worse. I don't have any luck. Nothing works out for me, and this won't either. I'm sure I'll get sick—or one of the kids will have a terrible accident." There was more, much more, of the same sort of junk.

Finally, we realized that Luann's depressing notions were a habit. We decided to try having Luann reward herself for telling herself the truth whenever she started rehearsing her Pandora's box of fake evils. Luann agreed to memorize something like the following:

- "Things are *not* sure to get worse. Getting better is just as likely as getting worse, and ultimately, God's work in my life will order everything to perfection.
- "There is no such thing as luck. God is in control, and I can think of all sorts of things that have worked out well in the past. I have His promise that He will work out everything for me in the future. Even if this project doesn't go the way I want it to, God knows better than I what's good for me, so I'm going to declare it's good, no matter what!
- "I have no reason whatever to be sure I'll get sick. God wants me whole and healthy. But even if He does let me suffer for a while, He can and will bring me through it better than before. He is my Healer.
- "I can just as well tell myself God is taking perfect

care of the kids and that nothing is an accident when He is in charge. I'm going to believe Him when He says He will protect us from harm."

She was to start rehearsing her memorized thoughts aloud whenever she caught her negative thoughts beginning to invade her mind. The new behavior was incompatible with the old thoughts. So the negative thoughts would have to give way. Luann was to repeat this as often as necessary to quite literally crowd the negative thoughts out of her consciousness.

When she finished and gained even a small temporary victory, she was to reward herself by permitting herself to read a chapter in a novel by her favorite Christian author, George MacDonald. For her, this was a top-grade reinforcer. Of course, she was not to allow herself to read MacDonald any other time than after successfully substituting her truthful thoughts for the old, Satan-inspired negative cognitions.

Luann soon noticed she was "motivated" to succeed by her desire to get back to her novel, and succeed she did. The negative thoughts faded quickly. Eventually, the new thoughts became automatic substitutes, habitual replacements for the old self-flagellating nonsense, and Luann enjoyed new feelings in place of her melancholy most of the time.

However, Luann soon found she had to make one change in her program. Soon after beginning, she noted that the more she succeeded in *keeping* negative misbeliefs out of her consciousness, the fewer opportunities she would have to read. We realized this *might* cause her to reintroduce the misbelieving cognitions to consciousness in order to fight them, win and get back to reading her novel. So we agreed on an important alteration. Luann was to allow herself *two* chapters before going to bed if she managed to get through an entire day without entertaining the old self-torturing beliefs at all.

Soon after this change was made, Luann began reporting days and even weeks at a time during which none of the unwanted ideas occurred to her. Needless to say, a change in her feelings followed as night follows day. At last, Luann knew sustained, contented feelings of spiritual and emotional wholeness.

HOW YOU CAN REWARD YOURSELF

You can reward yourself for successful efforts at changing any habit. Just be sure to make your plans carefully and prayerfully. Then, begin rewarding yourself *each time* you successfully refuse a cookie or a piece of candy, each day you turn down a chunk of the Danish brought in every morning for the gang at your office, every time you get up early on Saturday morning and mow the lawn, and so forth.

Perhaps you would like a list of things others have used as reinforcers or rewards. Remember, you must think of something rewarding *for you*. This list might start your thoughts in the right direction:

coffee or coke breaks
trips
movies
clothes
listening to records
reading favorite materials
time to sit and do nothing
cookies, candy, cake, other edible treats
tennis, bike riding, skiing
phone calls to friends
time with friends
visit to library, zoo,
planetarium, shopping mall
time with hobby

Be sure to observe the following rules when you use rewards:

1. Make certain the "reward" is really rewarding for you.

2. Give yourself the reward faithfully *every time* you perform according to the rules you set up.

3. Give yourself rewards you can enjoy immediately, not weeks, months, or years later. Giving yourself a new dress after you lose fifty pounds will not work very well as a motivator to get you to pass up *today's* piece of Danish.

4. Under no circumstances are you to give yourself the reward except when you have successfully fulfilled the conditions you set up.

5. Be willing to alter your program if you see it isn't working or if it becomes clear that its consequences include some unexpected, undesirable effects (as Luann did when she realized that success would prevent her reading her novel altogether under the terms of her initial program).

6. Be sure to record your program in your journal, and to keep records showing each reoccurrence of your habitual unwanted behavior and each success. You will thus have data you can count to determine how well your self-rewards are working.

If you have been having trouble with some especially persistent habit, pray for guidance. If it seems good to the Holy Spirit and to you, try introducing self-reward.

NEGATIVE CONSEQUENCES FOR UNWANTED ACTIONS

The Creator has so designed the universe as to build punishing events into it. Painful consequences often follow when we violate important laws of living. Think of the painful results of touching something red hot, inhaling liquids, going outside without enough warm clothing, or disturbing a contented wasp. We have all learned important lessons through punishment. God's law contains punishing contingencies for those who disregard it, and the Scriptures leave no doubt that good parenting involves some punishment training (Prov. 22:6, 15; 23:13, 14). You can use punishment effectively on yourself, too.

Fred was a psychologist. He was especially interested in changing behavior by rewarding the desirable and punishing the undesirable. So when Fred wanted to quit smoking, he decided to punish himself every time he had an impulse to reach for a cigarette.

Fred put a thick, strong rubber band around his wrist. Each time he became aware of an impulse to smoke, Fred snapped his wrist smartly with the rubber band. Each day, the number of times Fred felt like lighting up decreased. Although Fred used other habit-changing devices, this mild, but noticeable punishment helped.

Here are some punishers others have used to change their habits. You might consider using any of them or something else you think would change your own behavior. You could: deprive yourself of something you enjoy a lot, force yourself to get up a half hour earlier than usual, use mild, harmless pain (like Fred's rubber band or a small electric shocker you can carry in your pocket), or force yourself to apologize, or make amends to others.

Here are some rules to follow if you are going to use self-punishment:

1. Make sure the consequence you select really is punishing for you, that it is unpleasant enough so you'll change behavior rather than endure it.

2. Administer the punisher *each time* your unwanted behavior occurs. No exceptions!

3. Punish yourself immediately, or as quickly as you can after the undesirable habit occurs.

4. Do not punish yourself indiscriminately for every unwanted thought or action, but restrict your use of punishment to the one habit you are trying to break. One thing at a time is a good rule.

5. Be ready to change your program. You might find

it isn't working as anticipated. Try something different. Try a different punishing consequence, try administering punishment sooner, or try adding rewards for successes rather than relying only on punishing failures.

6. Record your program, keep track of numbers, and know whether you're getting results and why.

PRAY WITHOUT CEASING

None of the habit-changing techniques suggested in this book can work without God's blessing. That is true even for unbelievers making use of them. As His sun must shine even on the evil if their crops are to grow, so the sun of God's blessing can and does shine even on godless people using methods in line with God's principles, incorporated in His Word and in the design of His universe. Without God's sustaining blessing, no human effort would avail anything—ever.

Prayer, however, has special promise attached to it. God has promised that when believers pray according to His will and in terms of the covenant wrought through the blood of Jesus, results will follow. We can expect therefore that prayer before, during and after making efforts along the lines suggested in this chapter and throughout this book will produce measurable results, better results than could be gotten without prayer.

Pray for guidance and direction before you begin working on any habit-change program. Examine your heart before God. Make no effort to deceive Him before whom all hearts are open. Admit your mixed motives, confess your weaknesses and sinfulness; but also confess that Jesus has taken your sins away and filled you with the Holy Spirit. Confess the resulting power in your life. Expect that God will reveal His will and guide you as you consider taking action and make your plans.

Pray moment-by-moment as you work your program. Ask God to reveal any self-deception in your internal monologue, any misbeliefs with which you are preventing yourself from walking the way the Holy Spirit has mapped out for you. Ask Him to teach you the truth as you need to work it into your new, powerful self-talk.

Finally, when you have acquired a measure of self-control, when you have gained victory over some unwanted habit, praise and thank God. Don't be discouraged by slips or relapses. Instead, keep your eye on His promise: "The truth shall make you free," and begin again. And keep your eye in prayer on the perfection to which He has called you and which He will work in you according to His own promise.